D1524200

Why Blog?
Motivations for blogging

CHANDOS
INFORMATION PROFESSIONAL SERIES

Series Editor: Ruth Rikowski
(e-mail: Rikowskigr@aol.com)

Chandos' new series of books are aimed at the busy information professional. They have been specially commissioned to provide the reader with an authoritative view of current thinking. They are designed to provide easy-to-read and (most importantly) practical coverage of topics that are of interest to librarians and other information professionals. If you would like a full listing of current and forthcoming titles, please visit our website www.chandospublishing.com or e-mail info@chandospublishing.com or telephone +44 (0) 1223 891358.

New authors: we are always pleased to receive ideas for new titles; if you would like to write a book for Chandos, please contact Dr Glyn Jones on e-mail gjones@chandospublishing.com or telephone number +44 (0) 1993 848726.

Bulk orders: some organisations buy a number of copies of our books. If you are interested in doing this, we would be pleased to discuss a discount. Please e-mail info@chandospublishing.com or telephone +44 (0) 1223 891358.

Why Blog?
Motivations for blogging

SARAH PEDERSEN

Chandos Publishing

Oxford • Cambridge • New Delhi

Chandos Publishing
TBAC Business Centre
Avenue 4
Station Lane
Witney
Oxford OX28 4BN
UK
Tel: +44 (0) 1993 848726
E-mail: info@chandospublishing.com
www.chandospublishing.com

Chandos Publishing is an imprint of Woodhead Publishing Limited

Woodhead Publishing Limited
Abington Hall
Granta Park
Great Abington
Cambridge CB21 6AH
UK
www.woodheadpublishing.com

First published in 2010

ISBN:
978 1 84334 583 1

© S. Pedersen, 2010

British Library Cataloguing-in-Publication Data.
A catalogue record for this book is available from the British Library.

The Publishers make no representation, express or implied, with regard to the accuracy of the information contained in this publication and cannot accept any legal responsibility or liability for any errors or omissions.

The material contained in this publication constitutes general guidelines only and does not represent to be advice on any particular matter. No reader or purchaser should act on the basis of material contained in this publication without first taking professional advice appropriate to their particular circumstances. Any screenshots in this publication are the copyright of the website owner(s), unless indicated otherwise.

Typeset by RefineCatch Limited, Bungay, Suffolk
Printed in the UK and USA

Contents

Acknowledgements

I must firstly thank the Arts and Humanities Research Council (AHRC) and the Robert Gordon University Research Development Initiative (RDI) for funding parts of the research on which this book is based.

I am particularly grateful for all the assistance given to this project by Dr Caroline Macafee, both as a researcher on the RDI-funded research on British bloggers 2005–6 and for reading through and commenting on a draft of this book. In addition, I am grateful to my husband, Dr Frederik Pedersen, who also read and commented on the book. It goes without saying that any errors in the book are, of course, mine.

I would also like to offer grateful thanks to my students Alistair Chivers and Tracey Forbes, whose work on blogging has been interesting and beneficial to my own research, and Dr Janet Smithson of Exeter University for her collaboration on our online parenting communities project, which has expanded my understanding of the motivations of women online.

My grateful thanks to all the bloggers who generously responded to my surveys, commented on my blog and have allowed me to quote from their blogs.

I would also like to record grateful thanks for all their support to Professor Rita Marcella, Dean of the Aberdeen Business School, and Professor Dorothy Williams, Director of the Institute for Research in Management, Governance and Society, of which I am a member. I would also like to thank my colleagues in the Department of Communication, Marketing and Media for their support throughout the years, in particular Jo Royle, Dr Peter Reid, Nicola Furrie, Izzy Crawford, Dr Fiona Smith, Dr Robert Halsall and Tim Conner.

Finally, my repeated thanks to my husband Frederik and also to our sons Thomas and Nikolas for all their support.

About the author

Dr Sarah Pedersen is a Reader at the Department of Communication, Marketing and Media at The Robert Gordon University (RGU), Aberdeen, Scotland. She is also a member of the Aberdeen Business School's Research Institute for Management, Governance and Society.

Having previously worked as an editor in educational and academic publishing in Cambridge, she joined RGU in 1996 as a Lecturer in Publishing Studies. Her PhD investigated women's use of letters to the editor in Aberdeen daily newspapers 1900–18, and she has presented conference papers and published widely on this topic.

In recent years her interest in women's use of the media has moved to focus on computer-mediated communication. In particular, she has investigated women's use of blogging and the practices and motivations of British bloggers. In 2006–7 she was awarded an AHRC Research Leave Grant to research differences and similarities in practices and motivation between British and American bloggers. Her research has investigated the impact of the second wave of blogging on the blogosphere outside the United States and has pinpointed some important differences between the dominant American model and later blogging development elsewhere in the world. She is currently working on a research project focused on parents' use of the Internet with Dr Janet Smithson of Exeter University.

She served as Chair of the UK Association for Publishing Education (UK APE) from 2006 to 2010 and is a member of the advisory board for the International Conference on the Book and the *International Journal of the Book* and the AHRC Peer Review College.

She lives in a wooden house in Aberdeenshire with her husband and two sons where she surfs the Internet a lot.

The author may be contacted via the publishers.

Introduction

My first introduction to blogging was at a media history conference in California nearly a decade ago. On the first morning of the conference, I was walking through the host university's campus, admiring the brilliantly clear sky and the beautiful orange trees, on a hunt to find breakfast when I came across another delegate sitting cross-legged on a stone bench tapping away at his laptop. Having exchanged greetings and enquiries about the breakfast (he didn't know where it was arranged either), I made some passing comment about him desperately trying to finish his paper. No, he assured me somewhat smugly, the paper was all finished – he was 'blogging the conference'. In other words, he was writing about his experience at the conference by posting to his blog. His blog had a history theme, and was publicly accessible, but he aimed to write a mixture of subject-related matter and more personal posts. I had just interrupted him in a post about the beauty of the campus and the warmth of the day. He aimed to write a couple of posts a day, which would help his friends and family keep in touch with his activities while he was abroad, hopefully offer some useful information about current research to his students and also publicise the conference to those who might be interested.

It turned out that breakfast had not in fact been organised by the conference organisers and, on further investigation, that the oranges were horribly inedible, but I mostly remember this conference as the one where I was introduced to the fascinating world of the blogosphere. My colleague was a comparatively early adopter of a craze that was soon to sweep the world and I caught sight of him on several occasions during the conference explaining his activities to interested delegates – some of whom, like myself, may have left that conference determined to investigate the world of blogging a little more.

My own interest in blogging was piqued by the similarities I could already see between blogging and my own research interests at that time in correspondence to newspapers. I had been undertaking research into women's correspondence to newspaper editors during the early years of the twentieth century and was particularly interested in the way in which some women were able to use the 'Letters to the Editor' columns in newspapers to step out of their domestic setting and make their opinions about local, national or even international affairs known outside their circle of friends and family. The letters columns of local newspapers offered Edwardian women a place where they could safely access the public sphere and join in the public debate while feeling secure in their private sphere. The pen names that they chose (frequently referring to their status as wife or mother) and the way in which many of the letters were framed to discuss their chosen subject from a domestic point of view positioned these women on the cusp between the private and the public spheres. Given that local newspaper practices of that time meant that all letters sent to the editor were published as long as the correspondent's name and address were supplied (although they could request that they were not printed in the newspaper), women could even use the columns to discuss points of view and issues that were contrary to the stated opinions of the newspapers – the fight for women's suffrage being a frequent case in point in those years before the First World War. They were thus able to use their letters to the editor to engage in public debate at a time when the emergence of women from the home was both a controversial subject and a growing phenomenon (Pedersen, 2002a, 2002b, 2004). Were modern women (and men) now using their blogs to make a similar contribution to the public debate? The fact that bloggers have full editorial control over their blog and can reveal as much or as little about themselves as they wish might make blogging even more attractive than writing letters to newspapers for those who wished to contribute their voice to the public debate.

I was not the only one to make a link between blogging and the public's use of newspapers: many commentators in the media who were tasked with explaining the phenomenon of blogging in those early days made references to newspaper opinion columns and 'Letters to the Editor' that allowed members of the general public to 'blow off steam' about local or national issues in an informal yet public way. It was also exciting to come across such a useful source for accessing the opinions and thoughts of what could be described as 'ordinary citizens' rather than professional authors, politicians and others more familiar with debate in the public sphere.

My initial interest in blogging was therefore naturally focused on women's use of blogging and, in 2003, I undertook a small pilot study using content analysis to investigate 50 women's blogs. The analysis was particularly concerned with the stated motivations of these women for writing a blog, whether a change in motivation could be perceived over time and the audience (if any) for whom they considered themselves to be writing.

What is a blog?

It would probably be helpful at this point to give a short introduction to the blogosphere and offer some basic definitions of blogs, blogging and associated phenomena. Rebecca Blood, an early blogger and published writer on the phenomenon, offers a useful posting on the history of blogs on her blog *Rebecca's Pocket* (*http://www.rebeccablood.net/essays/ weblog_history.html*) and I recommend that anyone who wants to know more about the history of blogging start there. She tells us that we usually date the phenomenon of weblogs or blogs from 1998–9 and that weblogs were so named by Jorn Barger in December 1997, but quickly shortened to 'blog' within a few years. In 1997, Jesse James Garrett, the editor of the proto-blog *Infoshift,* started to identify and collect other sites that were similar to his own and his 'page of only weblogs' listed the 23 sites he had identified by 1999 (*http://www.jjg.net/retired/portal/tpoowl .html*). Again, in 1999, Birgitte Eaton compiled a list of every weblog she knew about and created the EatonWeb portal (*http://portal.eatonweb .com*). Other important prototype weblogs include Dave Winer's *Scripting News* and Rob Malda's *Slashdot*, both of which started in 1997.

Blogging was initially restricted to those who had the necessary programming skills and thus many of the early blogs were related to IT and the Internet in some way. However, with the introduction of cheap and easy-to-use build-your-own blog software such as Pitas and Blogger in 1999, it became possible for anyone with an Internet connection to create his or her own blog and this resulted in the explosion of the 'blogosphere' (the collective community of all blogs) over the first decade of the twenty-first century.

Blogs can be defined as 'frequently updated, reverse-chronological entries on a single webpage' (Blood, 2004). The original blogs were filter-type web pages, essentially editing the Internet for their readers, directing the reader to other blogs and websites and offering commentary and often the opportunity for readers' discussion, either with the blogger or among themselves. The main focus of these early blogs was on the links they offered – Blood refers to blog 'editors' rather than authors or writers and researchers such as Mortensen and Walker (2002: 265) were still describing blogs as 'focusing on connections and on brief nuggets of thought. Links are vital to the genre' in 2002. In comparison, the newer, so-called 'journal', blogs that arrived at the beginning of the twenty-first century focus more on commentary, which may also include links and reader responses depending on the theme and purpose of the weblog. Thus, with the popularisation of blogging, the web-bibliographical function has ceased to be the main criterion of blogs. Whereas filter blogs are heavily reliant on links to and from their site and the comments of readers, journal blogs tend to have smaller audiences, less reader participation and fewer links to other sites. In Herring et al.'s (2004) sample of 203 blogs, only 31.8 per cent contained links, which is a reflection of the prevalence of the personal journal blog in the sample (Herring, 2004a). It might also be argued that link-driven filter blogs tend to be focused on external events, whereas 'journal' bloggers write more about events in their own lives. However, it is important not to impose this filter/journal division too strictly when investigating the blogosphere since most bloggers use a mixture of styles, with filter bloggers discussing their personal responses to external events such as new software, wars or elections and personal journal bloggers recording and commenting on external events as well as on their own interests.

Although there were only 23 websites identified as blogs in 1997, with the introduction of easy-to-use software, the blogosphere grew quickly. In 2008, the blog-tracking directory and search engine Technorati claimed that it had indexed 133 million blogs since 2002 (Technorati: State of the Blogosphere, 2008). Of course, not all of these blogs are frequently updated and a high proportion of blogs are abandoned: Dave Sifry, the founder of Technorati, estimates that as much as 45 per cent of the blogosphere is made up of abandoned blogs (Sifry, 2005). Some are never used but are created as tests or as automatic features on social community sites such as MySpace or Bebo, which are particularly popular with teenagers (Henning, 2005). I have to admit my own responsibility here for some of these abandoned blogs – I have run labs in which I have asked an entire class of students to set up a blog in order to explore the phenomenon, and I expect that the majority of these have just been abandoned to float empty around the blogosphere once the class has been released. Huffaker found that 43 per cent of his sample of teenage bloggers had abandoned blogs (2004) and an increasing proportion of all blogs – according to Sifry about 9 per cent – are fake or spam (2006).

The arrival of the journal blog changed the nature of blogging. Although, among its practitioners, blogging is frequently characterised as socially interactive and community-like in nature, some research suggests that it is not so in practice (Herring et al., 2004a). Although journal blogs do discuss external issues and events, they often do so from personal perspectives. This may again indicate a growing number of women bloggers since, as Herring pointed out as far back as 1994, women who participate in discussion on the Internet tend to display a personal orientation. In addition, most of the journal blogs investigated in early studies of the blogosphere did not show high interactivity. Many had a fairly small set of regular readers and the bloggers might receive feedback on their blogs not just from such commentators but also in 'real life'. Nardi et al. (2004b) found that some blogs even facilitated in-person social contact, for example if the blogger was travelling. Although the 'A-list' blogs receive hundreds of comments a day, Nardi et al. (2004b) suggested that most journal blogs are read by only a few friends and that bloggers have 'regulars' who they know are reading their posts.

Nevertheless, in the past ten years, blogging has evolved from being a specialist niche activity, indulged in only by those with advanced programming skills and known about by only a select few, to being part of the global culture. In June 2008, Technorati was tracking blogs in 88 different languages. Teenagers, politicians, lawyers, journalists, comedians and stay-at-home moms all blog. Events have their own blog – as do institutions. The principal of my university uses a blog to communicate with staff and students. Blogging has been discovered by marketing and PR departments as a way of establishing a two-way dialogue with particular publics. As we will see, bloggers can even hope to make money through their blog. You can sell advertising on your blog, sell subscriptions to your blog, be paid for mentioning products or even be approached by newspapers or publishers impressed enough by your blogging to offer you a contract.

Early research on the blogosphere

As stated previously, my first investigation into the blogosphere took place in 2003, when it was a slightly smaller place – by April 2004, it was estimated that there were 1.3 million sites calling themselves blogs on the Web, of which it was estimated that about 870,000 were actively maintained (Schiano et al., 2004). At that time, blogging was not the recognised phenomenon that it is today and I usually spent the first part of any conversation about my research defining basic terms – which was a new experience for someone who had spent the previous six years researching 'women' and 'newspapers', neither of which had required half as much explanation. Words like 'blog' and 'blogosphere' were greeted with suspicion by the version of Word then on my university's computers and the online display of the conference papers and articles I started to write had red wiggly lines underneath so many words that the casual observer must have assumed that I was borderline illiterate. For a historian, it was also a new experience to be working in a discipline with a comparatively small and very recent amount of published academic research and also to discover that the 'experts' on blogging might not necessarily be found in universities. In 2002, Mortensen and Walker commented that there was a considerable amount of popular writing on blogs but to date no published research on the topic. Even in 2004, Susan Herring was stating that scholarship on weblogs was still in its infancy with little published literature as yet.

In my first blogging project, I undertook a content analysis of 50 women's blogs over a period of six months, focusing on the reasons for blogging given in these blogs. The blogs were selected using the randomising feature of the blog-tracking website *www.globeofblogs.com*, selected as a data source because at the time it was tracking a large number of blogs from diverse sources. The only criteria for the selection of blogs were that they were written in English and by a woman over the age of 18. Inactive blogs were as useful as active blogs for this research because the reasons for someone to cease blogging were also of interest. I found the 'About Me' section that most blogs offer of particular use in this research, but most blogs also offer an archive section in which previous posts can be accessed and the majority of the blogs selected for this study offered access to two or three years' worth of posts.

My focus on motivations was a legacy of my previous work on correspondence to newspapers and also a desire to evaluate how this new mode of communication was being used by women, particularly since some research in the United States suggested that women made up at least 50 per cent of all journal bloggers (Herring et al., 2004a). The limited amount of published academic research on the subject of blogging at that time tended to focus on the categorisation and characterisation of blogs or bloggers – for example Krishnamurthy (2002) proposed the classification of blogs into four basic types along two dimensions: personal versus topical and individual versus community. In addition, my research eventually came to focus on the British blogosphere. When I started my research on blogging, the majority of published research was based on the experiences and categorisation of American bloggers, although this was soon to be augmented by valuable works on non-English-language blogging and experiences outside the West. Given my (embarrassing) lack of language skills and my base in the United Kingdom, I decided to focus on the British blogosphere, evaluating UK-specific use of blogging and, in particular, comparing it to earlier research conducted in the United States. Much of the early basic characterisation of the blogger, for example the picture of him as a young, white university student or graduate, was established by research conducted by US teams such as those led by Susan Herring. For example, the findings of Schiano et al. (2004) (mentioned below) were based on ethnographic interviews and content analysis of blogs conducted in June 2003 with 23 bloggers, seven of whom were women. Schiano et al. stated that they felt that such a sample was representative since 'at this time bloggers are primarily current or recent students living in the US and blogging in English' (2004: 1144). I wished to explore whether such characterisations could be applied to other parts of the Anglo-centric blogosphere and whether British bloggers, for the most part members of a second wave of blogging rather than early adopters, could be categorised differently.

Some research on bloggers' motivations had been carried out by this time – as stated, mainly in the United States – so it could be used as a base against which to compare my own findings. For example, as part of the debate about the categorisation of blogs, Nardi et al. (2004b) suggested categorising blogs according to purpose, offering the following five basic purposes:

1. Documenting the author's life
2. Providing commentary and opinions
3. Expressing deeply felt emotions ('the blog as catharsis')
4. Working out ideas through writing ('the blog as muse')
5. Forming and maintaining communities or forums.

In the same year, this team of researchers also suggested the following motivations for journal blogging in particular:

1. As diaries and personal record-keeping
2. As a continuing chronicle or newsletter
3. As sharable photo albums
4. As travelogues
5. As news digests or newspaper op/ed columns
6. As a forum for ongoing work (Schiano et al., 2004).

Here, the team used familiar concepts – the diary, the newspaper column and so on – in order to explain blogging to non-bloggers. Such an approach has been criticised by some researchers, for example by boyd (2005a), who criticises both academics and the mainstream media for the use of metaphors like diary-writing and publishing when describing blogging. She suggests that when Nardi et al. used the title 'Blogging as a social activity, or, Would you let 900 million people read your diary?' for their 2004 journal article, it perpetuated a connection between blogging and diary-writing that many bloggers themselves reject. However she does admit that even blogging tools and services have used such descriptions in the past, with Blogger using terms such as 'push-button publishing' and Diaryland and LiveJournal embedding such terms in their names. We will investigate this debate further later in the book.

It was also possible to build on previous work undertaken on motivations for the use of other earlier Internet phenomena. Much of this work utilised uses-and-gratification theory: the assumption that users actively seek out different media and that media consumption can satisfy a variety of needs. As Kaye (2007) points out, the reasons for using a particular Internet resource can vary depending on how it functions and the types of interaction that it allows. Those Internet resources that allow two-way communication, such as blogs or bulletin boards, offer users different satisfactions from those offered by websites, which only offer one-way communication – the difference between broadcasting and partaking in dialogue between either two or many individuals or groups.

In particular, very relevant research had already been undertaken on motivations for the construction of personal home pages, which predated blogs on the World Wide Web. Papacharissi (2002) had suggested six motivations for creating a personal home page: sharing information, entertainment, self-expression, communication with friends and family, passing time and professional advancement. Her later (2007) work on blogging motivations agreed with Nardi et al. (2004a) that bloggers were primarily motivated by desires for personal expression and social interaction.

Most usefully, Clancy Ratliff, based at the University of Minnesota, was also undertaking research on women's motivations for blogging, asking questions such as: does blogging give women a sense of empowerment? Does it accomplish anything for women and feminism? Why do women find blogging attractive?

Research on the British blogosphere

A pilot study of 48 British bloggers was undertaken in the winter and spring of 2005–6 (I refer to this throughout the book as the 2006 study). It was financed by a grant from The Robert Gordon University's Research Development Initiative and I was joined on the project by a part-time researcher, Dr Caroline Macafee, from the Department of Information Management, whose assistance during this time was invaluable. In particular, we were interested in seeing whether blogging in the United Kingdom, which in general started somewhat later than in North America, reproduced the gender differences in blogging behaviour, and the gender inequalities in recognition that had been observed in studies based largely on American bloggers, thus shedding light, from a different direction, on some of the reasons that had been advanced for women having less influence and less popular success in this field.

Our sample of 24 women and 24 men was drawn from two blogrings, or directories, that allowed bloggers to identify themselves as British: Globe of Blogs and Britblog.com. In the case of the latter, which was organised geographically and offered the opportunity to select bloggers from a map of the United Kingdom, care was taken to select similar numbers of bloggers from each geographical area of the United Kingdom, including Wales, Scotland and Northern Ireland. The selected bloggers had to be individuals resident in the United Kingdom (and not obviously transient) and contactable by e-mail. While the majority of bloggers offer the possibility of being contacted through posting a comment on their blog, not all offer their readers the possibility of contacting them more privately through e-mail. Bloggers were selected until we had an equal number of men and women and their blogs were checked to ensure that they had posted within the previous month (in other words, that their blogs were current). The gender of the blog authors was determined through the names, photographs and information given in the blog postings such as references to 'my wife' or 'when I gave birth'. Blogs in which the gender could not be ascertained were discarded. In this study, we confined our sample to bloggers aged over 18. In the blogosphere at large, a very large proportion of blogs is written by adolescents. In purely numerical terms, teenage bloggers predominate: bloggers under 19 made up 58.3 per cent in Henning's (2005) figures, up from 52.8 per cent in 2003. This population of bloggers is usually studied separately, as the social dynamic of communication among adolescents is different from that among adults

(Huffaker and Calvert, 2005; boyd, 2005b, 2006; Kumar et al., 2004; Lenhart and Madden, 2005).

Three methods were used to collect data. Firstly, a questionnaire was sent to our selected bloggers via e-mail. This was designed to explore blogging practices, attitudes and motivations, drawing on previous literature and my own earlier study. The questionnaire included open and closed questions. (It should be noted that although 48 surveys were completed, not all of our respondents chose to answer all of the questions. Thus, when giving details of the responses in the book, I will sometimes also give the number of respondents for that question. This methodology will also be followed with the second survey administered in 2007.)

Secondly, a content analysis of the blogs allowed us to note characteristics of the blog that were visible to inspection. These included the age of the blog (in months), based on the starting-point of the archives; links in the blogroll; the number and nature of enhancements to the blog, such as site meters and logos or links for other blog services; if there was a site meter, whether visitor statistics were hidden and, where available, the average number of visitors per day. A classification of the blog's content was made on the basis of the ten postings prior to the submission date of the questionnaire. Unfortunately, in the short space of time during which data collection was underway, two blogs were closed down. The archives were cleared from two others, whereas one did not keep an archive. For all but one, we were able to base classifications instead on earlier postings (preserved on the Internet Archive Wayback Machine) or on later postings: we do not believe the content type had changed in the interim. The content categories that seem best to represent the sampled blogs were personal, opinion and politics, religion, criticism, work and business, information technology, creative work (including literary writing), lesbian sexuality and links and chance discoveries. Many blogs have a mixture of content, but it is not difficult to identify the dominant themes so long as allowance is made for most blogs having a fair amount of personal content.

Lastly, a third set of data was retrieved from a range of blog-monitoring sites. These included the Technorati ranking of each blog (if ranked); a figure for the number of inward links, averaged from Technorati and Blogpulse figures (over variable periods of time depending on the content of the blogs' feeds) and the number of outward links and images in the current feed, expressed as figures per 1,000 words, based on the data from SurfWax for 44 of the 48 blogs.

We also devised a measure of the technical sophistication of the blogs in the form of an impressionistic five-point scale. The different capabilities of different blog hosts were taken into account. For example, not all hosts give the facility to paste code into the template, which limits the scope to add enhancements. One blog was omitted from the classification as no information could be found about the software used. The scale is as follows:

- 1 = unmodified template;
- 2 = pasting into template (Blogger), adding images (Livejournal);
- 3 = adding artwork, deleting or modifying the 'About Me' section;
- 4 = redesigned template;
- 5 = custom design, unhosted blog.

The blogs were also assigned to one of three 'success' levels (top, middle or bottom) on the basis of the highest value among:

- the figure for daily traffic, where available;
- the figure for inward links;
- the Technorati rank (top 10,000, top 100,000, top million, or unranked).

As stated previously, the findings from this research are referred to throughout the book as the 2006 study. The study led to some interesting insights into the current state of the British blogosphere and some preliminary observations about how and why British bloggers blogged, which are discussed in detail throughout this book. However, any comparisons to the blogosphere outside the United Kingdom had to be based on the research of others. The next step was therefore to expand the research to include a comparison between British and American bloggers. A further research project was therefore carried out between September 2006 and May 2007 and supported by a research leave award from the UK Arts and Humanities Research Council (AHRC). Unfortunately, funding was not available for research assistance and I was therefore forced to 'go it alone' at this stage of the project.

Using a very similar survey to the 2006 study, 60 British and 60 American bloggers (equal numbers of men and women) were surveyed about their approaches to blogging, including blogging techniques, habits, motivations and rewards. At the same time, data were collected directly from the respondents' blogs and by means of online tools (Technorati, Surfwax and The Truth Laid Bear). The bloggers were again identified through the use of the blog directories Globe of Blogs and Britblog.com. Both directories offered the opportunity to identify a blogger's home county or state, which meant that it was possible to ensure a wide coverage of both countries. The majority of bloggers indicated whether they were male or female in their 'About Me' page on the blog. For those who did not, it was usually easy enough to ascertain their gender through their blog postings. If gender or location was not identifiable, the bloggers were not contacted to take part in the survey. Although the project was not concerned about sexual orientation, the final sample of bloggers contained one British woman respondent who identified herself as a lesbian and one American man who identified himself as a gay. In addition, one of the British men was a transvestite. It should be noted that, during the eight months of the project, two of the British women respondents actually moved to live in North America, which probably explains why they were interested in a survey about blogging in the United Kingdom and the United States.

In addition to the survey and blog analysis, a blog related to the research was established, giving first-hand experience of the challenges of blogging and also offering the opportunity for further data collection since the surveyed bloggers were invited to comment on the research as it was ongoing. (And comment they did!)

The primary research findings reported in this book are therefore based on a mixture of both qualitative and quantitative data taken from 168 survey responses and the content and textual analysis of the respondents' blogs conducted between 2005 and 2007 plus the analysis of another 50 women's blogs conducted from 2003 onwards. The field of academic research on blogging is a developing one and previous academic research projects on the subject have been on a similar, or smaller, scale, particularly when based on qualitative research methods. For example, Gumbrecht's (2004) interviews of 23 bloggers at or around Stanford University, Karlsson's (2003) study of seven American-Japanese online diarists, Schiano et al.'s (2004) ethnographic interviews with 23 bloggers, Huffaker and Calvert's (2005) sample of 70 teenage bloggers or Menchen-Trevino's (2005) interviews with 14 college student bloggers. Studies that included quantitative methods such as surveys have tended to be larger – again usually on the same scale as ours – Efimova's (2003) survey of 62 bloggers and 20 would-be bloggers, Trammell et al.'s (2006) quantitative content analysis of 358 Polish bloggers or Baker and Moore's (2008) survey of 134 MySpace users. Some larger studies have tended to be divided into a larger survey (quantitative) and a smaller qualitative approach, i.e. the study by Brady (2006) who surveyed 167 bloggers and conducted 24 interviews or the study by van Doorn et al. (2007) who collected quantitative data from 100 Dutch and Flemish blogs and then conducted a qualitative analysis of four of these, whereas others, such as Miura and Yamashita's (2007) online survey of 1,434 blog authors in Japan or the larger surveys conducted for Technorati or the Pew Internet and American Life Project, have tended to be mainly quantitative. Throughout the book, the primary data findings, both qualitative and quantitative, will therefore be compared with the findings and conclusions of other scholars in the field, including the aforementioned studies, noting where differences or similarities can be found. Although the sample is still too small for much statistical significance to be attributed to it, it is hoped that the combined quantitative and qualitative approach plus the reference to other scholarly research in the area will provide sufficient justification for my final conclusions.

The aim of this book

This book therefore aims to consolidate the findings of the three research projects outlined previously while focusing on the basic question of 'Why blog?' For the most part, the discussion focuses on personal rather than corporate blogs, although the data covers both filter- and journal-type blogs. I will also focus primarily on the British blogosphere, although comparisons will be made with American bloggers. Over the past decade, much more research has been conducted on the motivations of bloggers – both in the United States and elsewhere – and reference is made throughout the book to these findings. Subjects to be covered in this book include the blog as a diary or letters to the editor, blogging as therapy, blogging for friends and blogging for strangers, privacy issues, blogging as a form of journalism or publishing, blogging as political activism, blogging for profit and whether women and men (or Americans and Brits) differ in their reasons for blogging. I will also touch on professional blogging as a form of PR or citizen journalism, but these subjects are not the focus of this book, which mainly aims to interrogate the subject of what motivates ordinary men and women to blog.

2

The journal blog: a traditional form mediated by the Internet

> Blogs are a little more personal, and the etiquette is less defined: if a [bulletin] board is like a party, is a blog like your living room? A booth at a street fair? I think it's like a front porch: it feels like a part of your house; you put furniture on it, plants. But it's right there on the street and the only thing stopping someone from walking away with your hanging ferns is social convention. The sense of it being private and owned, well, that's illusory. (*The Leery Polyp*, 1 February 2005)

When is a diary not a diary? Perhaps when it's a blog. As we have seen, early bloggers tried to act as filters of the Internet, directing their readers to interesting information through links. Such links might be to other blogs or to different types of websites. The blogger sometimes offered commentary on the links and there was usually the possibility for the reader to make comments on the blogger's latest posting, but the focus of these early blogs was very much on their links. Such link blogs required a certain technical ability with computer programming, so it is not surprising that many of these early blogs were built around IT themes. Then in 1999 came the introduction of easy-to-use, cheap or free blogging software such as Blogger and the concomitant explosion of the blogosphere. Now it was possible for anyone to blog, despite their limited IT knowledge.

With the expansion of the blogosphere, link blogs were no longer the only type of blog available. In a report on blogging demographics for the Pew Internet and American Life Project, Lenhart and Fox (2006) stated that the most popular content for a blog was the writer's life and experiences, with 37 per cent of their sampled blogs focusing on these subjects. Technorati's *State of the Blogosphere* 2009 reported that 45 per cent of respondents blogged primarily about 'personal musings' –

with this figure rising to 53 per cent for the 72 per cent of respondents defined by Technorati as 'hobbyist' bloggers (as opposed to professionals and would-be professionals who expected to make money from their blogging).

The newer style of 'journal' or diary blogs was characterised more by the frequently updated text in the blog than by links to other parts of the Internet and was more likely to be focused on the blogger rather than external links. Indeed, Herring et al. (2004a) sampled 203 US journal blogs and discovered that only 31.8 per cent contained any links at all. Their research also suggested that journal blogging appeared to be particularly attractive to women and teenagers. Van Doorn et al. (2007) also made this link and suggested that in the journal blog we are confronted with an intersection between the traditionally feminine act of diarywriting and the traditionally masculine environment of ICT.

Blogs sit on the cusp of the public and private spheres in a unique way, with bloggers writing for both themselves and their audience. A blog is neither a completely private diary nor a polished and edited piece of writing aimed purely at a specific readership. Mortensen and Walker (2002) suggest that, just as Habermas conceived of the salon as existing on the borderline of the private and the public, situated in private homes but part of the public sphere, so do blogs. In his 2005 study of London bloggers, Reed made comparisons with street graffiti – the text left for strangers to read – or even just the act of standing on the street and shouting, exposing oneself through text to people you don't know. With their links to other parts of the Internet, blogs are anchored in the public sphere, and yet they are also safe spaces within which bloggers have total editorial control. It is therefore possible to compare blogs with other means of communication that appear to straddle both the public and the private sphere, such as letters to magazines or newspapers; the writings of some newspaper columnists; personal webpages and published diaries and letters.

The diary genre

Both the mainstream media and academic research frequently use the descriptions 'online diary' or 'journaling' to describe blogging. Such terms can be helpful to convey to readers who may never have seen a blog something of the quality of the genre. There is much that is familiar about a blog for a diary user – the chronological structure and the focus on personal experiences and opinions, particularly if the blog is a so-called 'journal' type blog. And it is not just commentators who associate blogging with diaries. As we have already noted, many blogging services such as Diaryland or LiveJournal make the connection too. But is a blog only an online diary, or does blogging offer its users more (communication with others; publicity) or less (lack of privacy; negative criticism) than a diary? In actual fact, there is a separate online diary tradition whose proponents can feel just as uncomfortable about being associated with blogging as bloggers can be when labelled 'diarists'. boyd (2005) expressed the frustrations of many bloggers when she described the use of such terms as misleading and problematic because, although they are not fundamentally wrong, they do not convey the full picture.

So how far are bloggers motivated to write their blogs because they see them as at least similar to the traditional diary? A Canadian living in London spent a good amount of time in her blog trying to work out precisely why she blogged, particularly because she is a television presenter and so as a public figure has issues about a possible invasion of her privacy. In one post, she described how she used to keep a diary from the age of 12, but stopped writing it ten years later when it was read by someone she thought she could trust. So, if she had privacy issues about others reading her diary, why did she write a publicly accessible blog that could be read by family, friends and strangers all over the world? The answer is that, unlike her diary, her blog was *designed* to be read by others.

> With blogging I can write a 'diary' with the intention of others reading it which a) satisfies my love and need to write b) in some way documents a bit of my life c) helps me reach a lot of people and d) is a bit of fun. (*Gia's blog*, 9 July 2002)

This description shows a classic mixture of motives for blogging and clearly demonstrates how, in the mind of a blogger, an online blog can differ from an offline, traditional, diary.

Researchers in the area of diary-writing (see McNeill, 2005; O'Sullivan, 2005; Serfaty, 2004) tell us that the origins of diary-keeping date to the early modern period in the West, with two significant factors being the spread of literacy and the impact of the Protestant Reformation. Not only were more people able to read, but silent reading became the norm, rather than reading aloud, which was more usual in the Middle Ages. It is suggested that silent reading helped the reader to meditate more clearly and in their own time on what he or she was reading and to form their own judgements. In the early modern period, both the Protestant and Catholic churches encouraged their congregations to read and meditate on the Bible and other devotional materials and to keep written accounts of their spiritual progress. Thus diary-keeping was very much seen as a spiritual and religious exercise. With the arrival of the Age of Science and the expansion of the theories and practices of accountancy and bookkeeping and also the growing popularity of the yearly almanac, diary-keeping also encompassed the more secular world, noting important events, natural occurrences and domestic affairs, although a bookkeeping methodology could also be extended to include the enumeration and analysis of sins and good deeds committed throughout a writer's day. The philosophers of the Enlightenment reinforced the secularisation of the diary genre, encouraging the further exploration of one's internal debates and deliberations through journaling.

By the nineteenth century, diaries had evolved into what O'Sullivan (2005: 60) calls 'sites of self-exploration, self-expression and self-construction'. The persona of the diarist was now the focus of the diary and the exploration of his or her character the main motivation for keeping a diary, although such introspection was frequently still of a confessional nature. Diary-keeping flourished with the sharp increase in literacy during the nineteenth century and the growth of the middle classes, particularly among middle-class women edged out of the public sphere and confined to the home with little to do but to write about 'what they knew' – in other words, their own lives and character. Girls, in particular, were encouraged to use diary-keeping as a means of self-discipline, and while a 100 per cent literacy rate was close to achievement in the UK by the beginning of the twentieth century, diary-keeping was still very much an upper- and middle-class occupation, and particularly associated with women and girls. This makes such diaries and personal reminiscences particularly helpful for those interested in researching what Jalland (1986) has called 'the history of the inarticulate' – conventional, middle-class women of the Victorian period. The last forty years have seen a tremendous growth in research in the areas of women's history and feminist criticism of English literature, and good use has been made of the products of women writers – both those products intended for a public readership, such as novels and women's magazine articles, and those intended for a more private readership, such as diaries and letters. Showalter (1989) has described a shift in feminist criticism during this period from what she calls a 'critique' of primarily male literary texts to 'gynocritics', or a study of women's writing, and a discussion of the androcentric critical strategies that have pushed women's writing to the fringes of the literary canon. Spender (1980) has argued that nineteenth and early twentieth century women writers who wrote for a public audience posed a potential threat to the status quo, with its distinctions between the male/public sphere and female/private – or domestic – sphere. She suggests that the status quo was re-imposed by the dominant (male) group by creating a distinction between male and female writing. More recently, Lopez (2009) has suggested that there are many similarities between female bloggers and earlier female diarists in the way in which they have been treated by the academy, with academic research mainly focusing on male proponents of such autobiographical writing. Recent research on women bloggers (e.g. Pedersen and Macafee, 2006; van Doorn et al., 2007) is helping to counteract such an imbalance.

The online diary

Laurie McNeill (2005) explains that 'diaries' began to appear on the Internet a few years before blogs arrived, typically developing out of personal home pages, usually – like the later blogs – the home pages of individuals already associated with Internet technologies. For examples of early online diaries, see the Online Diary History Project (*http://www. diaryhistoryproject.com/*), which offers some personal recollections of writers who started online journals before January 1998 on how and why they began journaling. Viviane Serfaty (2004) explains that online diaries became widespread in the USA from around 1995 as the number of households connected to the Internet increased and in 1997 Internet providers started offering free space for homepages – which is the same year that blogs began to appear. Daniel Chandler's work on personal home pages explored how their creators used such pages to construct identity, not just to publish information. He pointed out that the authors of some of these home pages were extraordinarily frank about themselves compared to what they might admit in face-to-face interaction with strangers and suggested that the medium of web pages offered possibilities for the presentation and shaping of self that could not be achieved face-to-face or on paper. He also suggested that home pages enabled their creators to think about their identity. Miller and Mather (1998) suggested that differences could be found between the two sexes, with men's pages being shorter and more variety in length and self-reference being found in women's pages. They also suggested that women made more mention of the reader and demonstrated more awareness of those who might be viewing their pages than men (cited in van Doorn et al., 2007: 145).

A certain amount of research into the motivations of those who created personal home pages has been undertaken. Papacharissi (2002) suggested that creators of such pages were motivated by a wish to share information, for entertainment, self-expression and a desire to communicate with friends and family, while Walker (2000) suggested that home page motivations were either intrinsic – to start to contact people on the Internet – or extrinsic – to maintain relationships already formed elsewhere (cited in Menchen-Trevino, 2005). However, investigating the blogosphere in 2004 and the growing popularity of blogs over personal home pages, the team led by Bonnie A. Nardi suggested that bloggers rejected home pages because they conceived of them as 'static' and more formal and carefully considered than blogs. They suggested that what drew creators to blogs rather than home pages was their rhythm of short, frequent posts.

Internet diarists did not, and do not, necessarily see themselves as bloggers. In her study of female Chinese-American online diarists, Karlsson found that many of these diarists made a sharp distinction between a blog and online journals. The diarists in her study were all users of 'Rice Bowl Journals', a large US-based webring and online journal directory. Many of the diarists featured both a blog and an online journal on their sites and Karlsson found that they used their blog for short, spontaneous notes and the online journal for longer diary-type entries, written with more care. To these writers, length was what separated the online diary from the blog and the diary was more important than the blog, with one interviewee comparing the blog to the background commentary that comes with a DVD – in other words a non-essential but occasionally interesting item. These distinctions between blogs and diaries echoed the early research of Mortensen and Walker (2002) into academics who blog. They suggested that, unlike diaries, blogs are suited to the shorter attention spans of the modern world, and that the spontaneity of writing immediately rather than offering carefully thought out arguments releases academic bloggers from the expectation that their writing has to be perfect and polished. In his study of London-based bloggers in 2005 Reed noted that, to his group of bloggers, both the blog and the 'I' that it depicted were seen to be works in progress, with the blog recording precisely how a blogger felt at a particular time and place rather than consciously meditating on events later as might be expected in a more traditional diary. Many in Reed's group of bloggers admitted to keeping hand-written diaries in the past, but in contrast to such diaries, whose entries were usually delayed, he found that blogs were valued for capturing a person's impressions almost as they occurred. Bloggers talked to him about the need to quickly 'vent' the brain, to expel 'disposable' thoughts and feelings or even to 'brain dump'.

While diary-keeping has been described, for example by O'Sullivan (2005), as the pastime of a privileged few, the blogosphere appears to offer a far wider and more diverse group of writers the opportunity to publish their life stories to a general public (although it should be noted that Technorati's *State of the Blogosphere* 2009 still reported that the majority of bloggers surveyed were highly educated and affluent). Blogs are just one possibility for online autobiographical representation on offer to the Internet user: webcams, photo albums, involvement with discussion boards, and social networking sites also offer the opportunity to share one's life and opinions with a mass audience in a way that has not been possible for the average non-celebrity before. However, this is where questions need to be raised about whether bloggers choose to write their diaries online in order to reach an audience or whether the journal-blog genre is chosen for convenience and the aim of the final product is still private and personal for the blogger. In the past, diary-writing was conceived of as a very personal exercise, offering the opportunity to explore one's character and possibly one's soul – what are the differences with today's blogs?

Many bloggers – and in particular journal bloggers – claim to be writing primarily for themselves. So what do they hope to achieve by their blogging? Certainly there are still links to the type of spiritual investigation undertaken by early diarists. In 2004 a female blogger on LiveJournal tried to understand why she had been posting mainly 'a lot of religious meandering and mental cud-chewing', concluding: 'So I'm writing all this as much to think through things, discover how my mind works and where my priorities lie, my thoughts and feelings, as to read it over again later with new eyes.' However, she immediately followed these musings with an acknowledgement of her readership:

> Unfortunately for you, dear readers, it means I'm writing to myself as the primary audience and you all as the secondary. So it might not be as interesting for someone else to read. And for that, my apologies, but I won't be changing the behaviour. You're more than free to skip it. (*Maewyn's Musings*, 18 August 2004)

Such a post – directed at a readership she obviously understands is reading her blog yet making it very clear that the blogger wants to use her blog primarily as a diary or spiritual journal – demonstrates the contradictions involved in such blogging.

Bloggers using LiveJournal as their blog provider seem to be particularly prone to considering their blog as a personal diary rather than written with an audience in mind. LiveJournal has several security options, including the most popular 'friends only' option, which hides a post from the general public so that only those on the blogger's friends list can read it, and a 'private' option that allows bloggers to restrict their readership even more, making their LiveJournal a purely private diary. It was noticeable in my projects that bloggers using LiveJournal were more likely to state that they had started their blog with the intention of using it as a private diary, although their motivations sometimes changed through time.

> I would like to think that I'm writing this solely for my own benefit. Many bloggers say the same thing – that having a live journal [sic] such as this one is somewhat therapeutic in nature and they don't care who reads it – they're doing it for their own benefit. I guess I thought when I started this that that would be the reason I wrote too. For my own benefit. But I have to be honest with myself. I'm an exhibitionist at heart. I want you to read me. I want you to care what I have to say. I long for your feedback and comments. (*Scooby Snax*, 30 October 2003)

Certainly, the blog draws on some of the fundamental characteristics of the diary – entries are posted in a regular, chronological manner and are focused on the blogger's experiences and opinions. Reed (2005) points out that, just like a paper diary, blogs are structured around 'I' narratives and present the life of a sovereign subject who has a continuous identity and a coherent history. Readers make the assumption, unless told otherwise, that the posts draw on the blogger's own life. Trammell et al.'s (2006) research into the Polish blogosphere suggested that the diary type of blog was the most popular in Poland and that, as blogging tools have become easier to use, blogs have moved from being tools of information management to self-expression and personal subjects. They found that in the Polish blogosphere posts on personal issues were often vague, focused on the emotions that a blogger had experienced rather than detailing the event that triggered them, and that this might cause problems for the reader's understanding, demonstrating that the blogger was writing more for him or herself than for their reader.

However, the inter-activeness of the blog – offering readers the opportunity to comment, giving statistics of how many readers the blog attracts and from where in the world, allowing readers to click through to other websites that the blogger is discussing – is demonstrably different from the more concrete form of the paper diary. A paper diary is a very static form, presented in chronological order. However, with the use of a blog's archives and links, the reader can construct their own reading path, moving backwards and forwards around and outside the blog, comparing the opinions and experiences of the contemporary blogger with posts that were made some time ago, as well as moving away from the blog entirely through any links offered either in the current posting or through the blogroll. Lopez (2009) suggests that blogs can be viewed as database narratives with individual entries being able to stand alone and not necessarily or intentionally connecting to other entries thematically or sequentially. Thus, through technology, the blog offers a different and more fluid experience for both its reader and the author than a traditional diary.

So blogs have some of the characteristics of diaries, but can offer both their writers and readers an enhanced and different experience. How far then did the bloggers surveyed in 2006 and 2007 conceive of their blog as a diary? One of the questions in the survey asked the respondents how they regarded blogging, with pre-set choices of: a form of journalism, publication, diary-keeping and creative writing. Respondents could choose one or more of the descriptions and most bloggers reported that they regard their blogging activity as a combination of at least two of the named categories, with diary-keeping and creative writing attracting slightly higher figures in both the surveys.

As can be seen from Tables 2.1 and 2.2, many bloggers were uncomfortable with our suggested choices and selected 'Other'. The other descriptions of blogging suggested included an outlet for creative work; a place to share; personal knowledge management; a specialist newspaper column; a marketing initiative and therapy; and these other definitions of blogging will be addressed later in this book. Interestingly, in the 2007 survey two British women dismissed the idea of a diary, preferring to describe their blog as a 'journal' while an American woman preferred the term 'family record'. Several of the comments, however, suggested that respondents were aware that 'other' bloggers – although not necessarily themselves – did see blogging primarily as a form of diary-writing or journaling:

> It depends why someone is doing it. I've never been a 'I got up today, fed the cat, read the paper and scratched my bum' blogger. ... Because, what do you write about the next day – 'I got up, scratched the cat, fed the paper and read my bum'? You tend to find that the bloggers who do that type of blog don't last too long – they run out of stuff to say. I suppose, with me, it's a sideways look at life – mine

Table 2.1	2006 Respondents' answers to the question 'Do you see blogging as a form of ...?' ($n = 48$)

	British male	British female	Overall totals
Journalism	15	13	28
Publishing	14	15	29
Creative writing	16	18	34
Diary	17	19	36
Other	11	11	22

Table 2.2	2007 Respondents' answers to the question 'Do you see blogging as a form of ...?' ($n = 120$)

	British male	British female	American male	American female	Overall totals
Journalism	17	17	17	17	68
Publishing	18	16	18	16	68
Creative writing	23	17	17	19	76
Diary	21	21	9	22	73
Other	9	9	5	9	32

and my family's life. Everything I write about is basically true, but sometimes I will sex it up a bit... . (*Male respondent*, 2006)

Others noted that their blog had originally started as a diary, but had changed as they continued to post:

Before my blog was used as an online journal of my daily life, this has now become a minor part of the blog and I am now mainly concentrating on technical issues and issues about blogging itself. This change has taken place as I realised I'd like more people tovisit my site, which wasn't happening with the diary blog, as I'm trying to make some revenue from it using advertising. Plus I also realised it was quite difficult to find information on certain topics so started blogging about them to fill the gap in the market. (*Female respondent*, 2006)

Mine started as a personal diary that I didn't intend others to read. I'm intending to make more use of it when I get time: project journal and some tutorials based on my experiences. (*Male respondent, 2007*)

In comparison, one female respondent who was very clear in her response that she had started and used her blog to promote her online business still commented:

I really like the record of my life which I'm starting to build up and the blog is forcing me to document/photograph more of it which will be fascinating in later years. (*Female respondent*, 2007)

This demonstrates that even the most marketing-oriented blog can also be used in a number of more personal ways by its creator – possibly even against their will, as the blog is described above as 'forcing her' to act in this way.

Slightly more female respondents to the surveys agreed that blogging had replaced their paper diaries – eight in 2006, in comparison to six men, and 18 (7 Brits and 11 Americans) in 2007 in comparison to eight men (split equally between the two countries). This is not too surprising given the strong cultural connection between women and diary writing – Laurie McNeill (2005) refers to the diary's offline reputation as a 'feminine genre of no consequence'. Walker (2005) reflects on Serfaty's (2004) description of blogs and diaries as simultaneously 'mirrors and veils', both associated with the feminine, and points out that when a man is depicted as using a mirror he is likely to be shown doing something practical, such as shaving. Thus, she suggests, blogs kept for practical purposes might be considered more masculine than the more feminine diary blogs. This may also be the reason for some male bloggers' rejection of the idea of the blog as an online diary, particularly those who wish to see themselves as participating in a new and innovative cultural form. However, van Doorn et al. (2007) suggest that the blog is actually introducing a group of men, who would not think to write a paper diary, to the act of diary-writing online.

The results of the surveys, therefore, suggest that, while bloggers understand the concept of the blog as an online diary, they did not exclusively think of their blogging in these terms, and even those bloggers who had started their blog with the intention of keeping it as a diary had found that their blog had developed away from the original diary form. Such development usually came in response to readers' comments and feedback and it is such feedback that offers the essential distinction between diaries and blogs. Whether or not an offline diary was written with only the author as reader in mind or whether it was written with an eye to posterity and future publication, it is unlikely that the writer expected comments on his or her daily entries. Yet this is the essence of a blog – feedback from and knowledge of its readers, and such feedback often influences the way in which a blog is written and the thoughts and opinions of its creator.

Thus the concept of the blog as a type of online journal or diary is attractive to some bloggers, particularly women. Female identification with the idea of the blog-as-diary is not unexpected given the feminisation of the genre in the last two centuries. However, men can also be found using the blog as an online journal and it may be that, by combining online communication with the more traditional genre, the blog offers men the opportunity to experience diary-writing without the feminine connotations of a traditional diary. Having noted this trend, however, it must be accepted that there are more female 'journal' bloggers than male and women bloggers are more comfortable with conceiving of their blog as a diary or journal than are male bloggers. Thus the diary motivation appears to be predominantly a female one. Why then do such women go online and write their diaries in public? What does the blog offer them that a more traditional paper diary does not? The answer appears to lie in the extra facilities that a blog offers – the opportunity for making connections with a readership, to receive feedback from such readers, and the way in which these readers can navigate around the blog, creating their own journeys through the different postings, links and comments in a way that would be impossible with a traditional diary.

3

The journalism motivation

As mentioned in the previous chapter, the survey respondents were asked whether they considered blogging to be a form of journalism, publishing, creative writing, diary-keeping or other. The respondents were allowed to choose any number of these descriptions in combination. In 2006, 28 out of 48 (roughly equal numbers of men and women) stated that they saw blogging as a form of journalism, while in 2007, 68 out of 120 (again equal numbers of both gender and of Americans and British) agreed with this definition. In the eyes of the respondents, the concept of blogging as a form of journalism had equal merit with the other possible descriptions. Just as we saw with the idea of the diary, the definition of blogging as a form of journalism has also been popular with mainstream press commentators and academic researchers when faced with the need to explain the phenomenon of blogging to a wider world, although the journalism description tends to come with the words 'amateur' or 'citizen' attached to it in order to differentiate blogging from the older tradition – additions that are not seen as necessary when using the diary metaphor. Again, boyd (2005a) voices reservations about the use of this metaphor, stating that a description of blogging as just journalism and diary-writing or even as a combination of the two fails to capture its essence.

There are several ways in which blogs can be compared to journalism – and one of the most important is in connection with the motivations of their authors. Some bloggers are attracted to blogging because it offers them an opportunity to publish their opinion on topical news, possibly offering a different perspective or more in-depth material than is offered by the mainstream media. On occasion, news stories have even been broken by bloggers, and it is certainly true that journalists have learned to monitor the blogosphere for new angles or insights about a particular story. For the most part, however, blogs tend to be associated more with the opinion side of newspapers than with the provision of breaking news.

This chapter investigates the similarities in motivation between bloggers and journalists. Given that this book's focus is on the motivations of individual bloggers, and particularly British bloggers, it is not intended as a comprehensive analysis of the phenomenon of citizen journalism, which can be found in other, more in-depth, discussions on the subject (e.g. Gillmor, 2006). Instead, we will focus on specific blogging motivators that can be associated with the wider concept of journalism, including a desire to let off steam, to make opinions widely known, to influence the thinking of others and to engage in debate. It is these elements of blogging in particular that have led blogs to be described as similar to newspaper opinion columns and editorials or newspaper letters columns. We will also briefly touch on the way in which the mainstream media itself has been motivated to embrace blogging in response to such so-called 'citizen journalism'.

Letters to the editor

Letters to the editor of traditional or online newspapers can be valuable tools for journalists, giving them an insight into which topics are stimulating grass-roots debate, offering the possibility of dialogue between the newspaper and its readers and also providing the readers with a place to put forward their opinions or vent their frustrations. Writing a letter to the editor requires little special training and thus, in theory, is accessible to both the 'man on the street' and the expert, although selection by the editor can not be guaranteed for either and clearly letter-writing is limited to those who have the skills to shape a letter and marshal the necessary arguments to make their point (Smith et al., 2005). Although the majority of writers of letters to the editor are deemed to be occasional writers, reacting to a specific topic that has attracted their attention, more recent research has confirmed what the editors of letters pages have long known by identifying a group of regular writers, a minority of whom are fixated on one single topic. This small group may be perceived by newspaper editors to be mad, obsessional or even dangerous (Raeymaeckers, 2005; Wahl-Jorgensen, 2002). It should be noted that another section of letters comes from orchestrated media campaigns by particular social or political pressure groups – referred to by some journalists as 'astroturf' because of the fake grass-roots nature of such letters (Reader, 2008).

Only a limited amount of academic research has been undertaken on letters to the editor, and of that research, an even more limited selection has focused on the motivations of correspondents. During the 1970s, US researchers attempted to define the average letter-writer to newspapers, in particular during presidential election periods (Buell, 1975; Grey and Brown, 1970; Lander, 1972; Volgy et al., 1977). They tended to use evidence gathered for other purposes by bodies such as the Center for Political Studies and, because of the nature of this evidence, focused on the writer of letters on political subjects. From such research, the average letter-writer emerged as predominantly white, male, middle-aged or older, with an above-average education and income. Different groups of researchers found him to be a liberal Democrat voter or a Communist-hating, CIA-supporting Republican. However, all agreed that his interest in politics was above average and he was more likely to participate in other political activity than the average registered voter. Although the age range is different, there is a similarity here to the descriptions of the average blogger. Early research suggested that bloggers were primarily current or recent students living in the United States (or Western Europe) and blogging in English (Schiano et al., 2004). The characteristics of bloggers did not appear to significantly differ from the demographics of users of other public Internet communication tools; in other words, young adult men residing in the United States. More recently, Technorati's *State of the Blogosphere 2009* reported that two-thirds of the respondents to its survey were male, 75 per cent had a college degree and 40 per cent had a graduate degree, although other research on American bloggers has suggested that, in fact, half of journal bloggers are female (Herring et al., 2004a). As we have seen, female bloggers are more likely to write a journal- or diary-type blog rather than use their blog to publish more widely their opinions about external events and, at least in the mainstream media, political bloggers tend to be characterised as male. For instance, in 2006, an article on 'top blogs' in *The Independent* mentioned six bloggers, four of whom were male (Caesar, 2006), while a similar article in *The Guardian* on the top British political bloggers mentioned seven bloggers, six of whom were male (Burkeman, 2005).

Several basic motivations for writing letters to the editor of a newspaper have been identified. The primary motivation is, of course, the wish to participate in public debate by sharing opinions and experience. Other letter-writers might be driven by an impulse to educate the public or to call for action on a particular problem. Many letters are triggered by another letter or piece of editorial in the newspaper and might thus be seen as 'secondary' letters (Smith et al., 2005). In addition, letters to the editor can be seen as a kind of 'safety valve', allowing angry or upset readers to 'get something off their chest' in a harmless but therapeutic way. Linked to this motivation is the fact that many letters are written in a negative tone, rather than a positive or neutral one. Other common reasons for writing include requests for information or clarification and warnings. Just as for blogs, more than one motivation can be found in most letters (Pounds, 2006).

Again, comparisons can be made here with the blogosphere. The linking that is such an essential part of the filter blog can be compared to the way in which letters to the editor are triggered by material reported earlier in the newspaper. Bloggers' posts can be triggered by material found elsewhere on the Internet – either on other blogs or among the online presence of mainstream media. Thus, blog posts can be seen as a more immediate response than letters to the newspaper editor – and a response that does not have to rely on acceptance and selection by the editor. An overall negative tone can also be found in the blogosphere. Asked whether they agreed with the statement, 'I use blogging to vent my emotions or frustrations', 33 out of 48 respondents in the 2006 survey and 44 out of 90 respondents in the 2007 survey agreed that they 'sometimes' used their blogging in this way. In their answers to open questions about motivations, several of the respondents mentioned using their blogging as a way to 'vent' or 'blow off steam' about issues (and it was interesting to note how many times the idea of blowing off steam about issues arose in the respondents' answers, suggesting that they had bought into certain frequently used definitions of blogging current in the mainstream media):

'A way to let off steam!' *Male respondent, 2006*

'Release ... let off steam' *Female respondent, 2006*

'It allows me to 'vent steam' about things which matter to me.' *Male respondent, 2006*

'A vent for frustration' *Female respondent, 2007*

The concept of 'blowing off steam' also suggests a certain subjectivity in the way in which a blogger writes about a topic. Such a subjectivity is certainly a difference between the blogosphere and the mainstream media, which (at least officially) aims at objective reporting and reserves subjectivity for editorialising. Readers of news-related blogs can appreciate the way in which blogs represent the personal opinion, and even the emotions, of the blogger rather than a corporate line. Investigating why readers read news blogs, Pedersen and Chivers (2007) found that it was the personal content, tone and language of a news blog that kept readers returning to the site and this was favourably compared to mainstream news sites. Although acknowledging that blogs were subjective sources of news and commentary, the readers did not see this as a failing. Instead, they compared bloggers' open and avowed subjectivity – often termed 'passion' – favourably to what many perceived as a pretend-objectivity on the behalf of the mainstream media.

Although most researchers on newspaper letter columns felt that such a 'safety valve' role was harmless and ineffectual, Byron Lander's (1972) research on letter-writing following the shootings of the Kent State students in May 1970 suggested that such letters could have an effect on the political environment in a community. Although the editorials of the *Kent Record Courier* and a minority of letter-writers expressed horror and shock at the shooting of students on their own campus by the National Guard, the majority of correspondents did not follow the editorial lead of the newspapers. Instead, their letters were over-whelmingly hostile to the students and called for further repressive action. Lander suggests that such a response went well beyond the 'harmless safety valve' function since such an open approval of the killings could encourage further action against the students in the future. In this case, he suggested, letter-writers could well have been shaping future events by their encouragement of the National Guard's actions.

A couple of respondents made the same links as Lander's in their comments that blogging was 'mob violence for cowards' (male respondent, 2006) and 'political shin-kicking and eye-gouging' (male respondent, 2007), suggesting that contributions to debate, whether they are in the newspapers or online, are not always necessarily positive ones. The survey respondents were asked whether they agreed or disagreed with the statements given in Table 3.1 (page 32), designed to investigate whether their blogging might sometimes be a disagreeable experience.

As can be seen from Table 3.1, only a small minority of bloggers (equal numbers of men and women for both years) felt that they became upset because of heated exchanges and a larger minority actually gained stimulation from such exchanges. However, a larger group for both surveys agreed that they had experienced feedback that seemed intended only to cut them down. Presumably, however it might be *intended*, such a feedback upset only a small minority of the respondents and did not impact on their decision to continue with their blogging – at least in the short term. Thus, the respondents did not seem to equate blogging with hurtful argumentation and only a minority equated it with stimulating argumentation either. This is interesting when compared with the larger group that stated that they used their blog to vent their emotions and

Table 3.1	Responses to statements about the disagreeable side of blogging	

Statement	Agreement in 2006 (n = 48)	Agreement in 2007 (n = 91)
'I get upset by blogging because I get involved in heated exchanges'	5	6
'I gain stimulation from blogging because I get involved in heated exchanges'	15	14
'I have experienced feedback that seemed intended only to cut me down'	26	30

frustrations and thus it must be concluded firstly, that such a venting was usually connected to personal rather than external issues and, secondly, that it was usually not responded to by commentators on their blogs in a negative way – or not responded to at all.

Interestingly, there seems little suggestion in the academic literature on the subject of letters to the editor that the appearance of blogs has caused the number of letters to the editors of print newspapers to fall. In fact, an increasing proportion of readers appear to be writing such letters and it is suggested that new technologies such as e-mail and the Internet have rather helped improve the topicality and speed of response of such letters instead of diverting them to other online media (Raeymaeckers, 2005).

Making your voice heard: citizen journalism

Letters to the editor of a newspaper can provide researchers with a useful 'thermometer' with which to measure the amount of 'heat' – in terms of critical debate and discussion – a particular issue is arousing in the locality (Foster and Friedrich, 1937). In particular, research into the contents of correspondence columns in local newspapers can offer a different perspective from which to approach issues usually examined on a national or regional basis. In a similar way, the team led by Mike Thelwall has undertaken interesting research on bloggers' reporting of and reaction to events such as the London bombings and the Danish cartoon controversy, demonstrating that blog search engines offer a unique retrospective source of public opinion (Thelwall, 2006; Thelwall and Stuart, 2007; Thelwall et al., 2007).

One motivator for blogging can be a desire to redress perceived distortions or failures in the mainstream media and this view of the blogger as a kind of 'fifth estate', monitoring and commenting on the output of the news media, is perhaps the most familiar image of the blogger served up to us by the media. Such a picture usually makes reference to the bloggers who are credited with bringing down Senator Trent Lott and the A-list blogs such as *The Huffington Post*, *Instapundit .com* or *The Daily Dish*, which may be staffed by a number of full-time bloggers or citizen journalists and are seen as being particularly influential in, for example, American politics. Although blogs may only be read by a minority of the American public, certain blogs are particularly influential because of their interaction with national mainstream media (Adamic and Glance, 2005), with a high readership among journalists and other political elites (Drezner and Farrell, 2008).

Blogging as journalism or as a form of reporting has been a much-debated topic. Commentators such as Dan Gillmor (2006) see bloggers at the forefront of a revolution whereby a new breed of grassroots journalists is taking the news into their own hands. Gillmor's Centre for Citizen Media (*http://citmedia.org*) supports what is described as 'citizen or grassroots journalism' as a way of encouraging participation in current events by an educated populace. 'Citizen journalism' describes a form of media that involves moderated reader participation and is a response to what critics such as Gillmor see as the 'one-way journalism' of the twentieth century. Citizen journalism sites seek out people in the local community to write contributions and are happy to interweave opinion with fact. Such sites tend to be multi-authored but may involve editorial guidance and moderation. Not all blogs can be described as citizen journalism blogs, particularly because few single-authored blogs are editorially moderated, but these two forms of online writing do share some characteristics, such as the personal, opinionated nature of some of the writing and the ability to focus on a particular aspect of a news story. Blogs offer their readers an ability to interact with and discuss the news, to follow sources and to have world and local events filtered to remove material that is not of interest to them. Blogs also offer their readers expertise in areas that may not be of interest to, or are not covered widely in, the mainstream media. The back story of a particular event can be explored in detail and opinions from a number of viewpoints can be given. In addition, blogs, and now the micro-blogging phenomenon Twitter, offer the possibility for anyone at all to broadcast news to the world whenever they see it happening without having to go through official news channels, where they might possibly meet with delays, editorial interference or even censorship (Shirky, 2008: 186).

Mainstream media response

One way in which the mainstream media has responded to the possible threat posed by alternative news sources such as blogs has been to increase audience participation in the journalism process, particularly online. Using an 'if you can't beat them, join them' approach, many mainstream media newsrooms now employ staff to edit, manage and write their own interactive online content. Such a content can include chat rooms and forums, the provision of journalists' e-mail addresses so that readers can 'talk back', links to sources and personalised news selection on the Web. Many have also set up blogs in which individual journalists can write in a more personal way, albeit still as employees of the company, about their take on a particular news story. By 2007, 95 per cent of the top 100 US newspapers offered at least one reporter blog and, in the United Kingdom, the number of blogs in leading newspaper websites jumped from seven in 2005 to 118 at the end of 2007 (Hermida, 2008). Hermida suggests that, for the BBC, the push to adopt such blogs came from a need to win the public's trust back after a period of turmoil in 2004, when its reputation for accuracy and impartiality was questioned. It also fulfils demands for accountability, as 'Letters to the Editor' pages are deemed to do for print newspapers (Raeymaeckers, 2005). But at the same time, the BBC is seeking to normalise blogs within existing journalistic frameworks. Such an activity shows how journalists are striving to stay as gatekeepers, 'normalising' the blog as 'a component, and in some ways an enhancement' of traditional journalism (Singer, 2005).

For some journalists, blogs offer a chance to say what cannot be said on the news page or in a brief three-minute report to camera or to be creative beyond the newsroom – they can represent 'an assertion of the value of the personal in the public sphere' (Matheson, 2004: 452). Kahn and Kellner (2004: 93) argue that the commentary on and contribution to news stories by blogs has revolutionised journalism, giving non-journalists 'the realm of freedom, community and empowerment'. In her discussion of the use of blogs during the second US war with Iraq in

2003, Wall (2005: 153) suggests that blogs are a new genre of journalism that 'emphasizes personalization, audience participation in content creation and story forms'. She also argues that such characteristics suggest a move away from the modern approaches of journalism and that this new form can be seen as post-modern. However, Lowrey and Anderson (2005) suggest that the consequence of such audience participation in the journalism process may be a further weakening of the mainstream media's exclusive authority in the eyes of the public and that the more audiences use the Internet in participatory ways to obtain news, the more likely they are to think that they could master the journalism knowledge base. In particular, with a broadening of the definition of journalism to include commentary and opinion rather than straight fact reporting, the traditional concept of news is being blurred and redefined to include the use of alternative sources such as blogs.

On the positive side, blogging can offer opportunities for professional journalists to 'keep their hand in' during periods of unemployment. One of the respondents to the 2007 survey had been a newspaper columnist at her local paper in the Shetland Islands, writing mainly about events in her local area. When the paper folded, she was encouraged by her readers to carry on her column as a blog. Another respondent, a freelance journalist based in New Hampshire, United States, used her blog to help her 'keep track of what I've written for the local newspapers, with links to the articles and columns ... and I share them with a wider audience than would read them in print'. Interestingly, she found that her blog had grown to become more personal – 'because people like to read that and I like to write it'. Thus, these two journalists had found that their blogs offered them an opportunity to both expand their readership and offer their readers what they wanted and what the journalists themselves wanted to write, whether or not they were commissioned by an editor. There was also the possibility that a particular story might be picked up by an editor and that they would be commissioned to write a piece based on a blog post, which had happened to the New Hampshire journalist: 'One of my editors has read things I've written and suggested articles for the Sunday newspaper'. Technorati's *State of the Blogosphere 2009* reported that 35 per cent of its respondents had worked at one point in their lives in the traditional media, for example as reporters, writers, producers or on-air personalities, whereas 27 per cent of respondents were currently both bloggers and workers in the traditional media.

However, the participatory nature of blogs can offer additional challenges that not all journalists are keen to embrace – and motivation can be a key factor in how committed journalists are to their blogs. Schultz and Sheffer's (2007) investigation into the motivations of US sports journalists who blogged made a clear distinction between those journalists who blogged because they had a personal commitment to the new media and those who were impelled to blog by their employers. Of their sample of 124 sports journalists, only 27 per cent had initiated the idea of a blog themselves and 52 per cent had been told to blog by management. There were significant differences between the group motivated by management and other groups, with this group being more likely to view a lack of training as a problem, less likely to believe that blogging made them better journalists and less likely to believe that blogging had increased the size of their audience. It tended to be the journalists with more than ten years of experience who were reluctant bloggers, and this group was also more likely to be concerned about issues of credibility and ethics related to blogging. Schultz and Sheffer reported a feeling among these older journalists that media managers had rushed into blogging without a good understanding of how it worked or the dedication of resources to make it effective. Such a reluctance to join the blogosphere may explain why some media sources choose to employ bloggers themselves rather than encourage journalists to embrace blogging. For example, in March 2004, *The Washington Monthly* hired Kevin Drum, a *CalPundit* blogger who had been attracting over 1.2 million unique visits per month to his blog, to write a blog on its website entitled *Political Animal* (Drezner and Farrell, 2008). One of the respondents to the 2007 survey explained how she was approached by a newspaper company after her blog of film reviews became a popular hit on the Internet:

> It started out as a leisure time activity and has become my work. The postings on my blog are the same as the reviews that now appear in my syndicated column of movie reviews, which appear in various newspapers across the Northeast [of the US], thanks to a deal made with a company that saw the work on my blog and hired me to be their critic.

Redressing the mainstream media

The research discussed in this book is more focused on individuals who saw themselves as bloggers rather than citizen journalists. Having said this, some of the respondents did see part of their motivation in blogging coming from a desire to comment on or even to influence public opinion

Table 3.2 What satisfactions do you gain from blogging?

Satisfaction	2006 participants (n = 48)	2007 participants (n = 100)
You are exercising your talents	35	74
You are displaying your talents	20	56
You are obtaining recognition of your talents	19	46
You are sharing your expertise	17	53
You are sharing your specialist knowledge	18	49
You are sharing your wisdom	23	44
Writing helps clarify your thinking	39	79
You are participating in a democratic movement	15	26
You are helping to redress the distortions and inaccuracies of the mainstream news media	12	30
Other reason	19	23
No satisfaction	0	1

on political matters and possibly to redress the reporting of such matters in the mainstream media. However, this was a motivating factor for only a minority of the participants. In listing the satisfactions that they obtained from blogging, 12 respondents in the 2006 survey and 30 in the 2007 survey agreed with the statement that they were redressing the distortions of the media and similar numbers (15 in the 2006 survey and 26 in the 2007 survey) agreed that they gained satisfaction from blogging because they were participating in a democratic movement, but, overall, these were much less popular choices in comparison with other options (see Table 3.2), suggesting that for these respondents, at least, their blogging satisfactions were mainly related to internal rather than external impact.

However, explicit connections were made by some respondents, mainly men, between their blogging and the role of the 'fifth estate' – to keep an eye on the mainstream media as well as politicians. One male respondent, on being asked why he blogged, tersely replied: 'Rupert Murdoch'.

Another stated:

> I blog to hold politicians to account, to campaign for local issues, and to air views which the local press are afraid to broach (the local council is a rich source of news and the newspaper does not wish to lose its access by being critical).

He also claimed that 'I am influencing the decision-making process within our local council. My blog has many influential readers including journalists, councillors, council officers, and members of parliament' and that 'disclosing information caused trouble for local politicians and held them to account in a more immediate manner!' Others saw blogging as an opportunity to influence public opinion on issues that were important to them:

> 'A contribution to debate, a voice of dissent from the predominant culture, a way of influencing thought not possible in other ways.' *(Male respondent, 2006)*
>
> '[I blog] when news happens and/or to comment when I feel I have something to add to the greater societal discussion.' *(Male respondent, 2007)*

However, for the majority of the respondents, blogging about external, political events took second place to blogging about their own lives and experiences. Neither were they alone in this navel-gazing. In their investigation of the Polish blogosphere, Trammell et al. (2006) comment, in some surprise, on the lack of interest their sample of Polish bloggers paid to issues outside their own experiences. Their research sample included posts written during the time of the enlargement of the European Union and Poland's accession to the European Community, but these events did not receive any attention from the bloggers analysed, who preferred to blog about their own lives and experiences instead. It thus seems that, despite the coverage in the mainstream media about citizen journalists and the impact and importance of political bloggers, these remain a small sub-section of the blogosphere. When investigating the 'long tail' of the rest of the blogosphere, we generally find more personalised motivations and interests. Although the respondents were happy to see blogging as a form of journalism, just as it might be a form of creative writing, diary-keeping or publishing, it seems that this association had a personal impact on only a very few of them and that, for the most part, the respondents were not eager citizen journalists motivated by a desire to keep politicians and the mainstream media on the straight and narrow. Instead, their view of blogging as a form of journalism seems to have been influenced by media coverage of the A-list blogs' perceived news agendas and the blogs provided by mainstream media sources rather than their own personal experience of blogging.

Blogging politicians

If we are investigating the motivations of those who blog in order to influence the opinions of others, then we might briefly want to consider the motivations of those UK politicians who blog. Politicians who blog first attracted attention when Howard Dean made use of a blog in the US presidential primaries in 2003 and this was also the year when the first British MP Tom Watson (Labour) started a blog. His stated motivation was not, as Dean's was, to use the blog as any sort of campaigning tool. Instead, Watson proposed to use the blog to make himself more accountable to his constituents. Jackson (2008) agrees that the limited number of British politicians who do blog do not choose to do so in order to campaign. His research into seven MPs' blogs in 2005 suggested that MPs were attracted to blogging because they hoped it would give them a more human, personal face and that the blog would be a useful tool to establish dialogue between themselves and interested members of the public. There has also been the motivator of external pressure from organisations such as the Hansard Society. However, Jackson suggests that the readers and commentators of such blogs may not necessarily be members of the MP's own constituency but rather members of a new 'e-constituency' that can grow up around the blog. Thus, blogs might help MPs to gather information and develop their policy ideas in specialist fields, but might not help them in their communication with their original constituents – and such a division between these two constituencies, one online and one offline, might lead to problems.

It is worth noting here the reasons why some MPs choose not to blog. Nineteen MPs told Jackson that they had considered blogging and decided against it, firstly, because of the pressure of time – they did not believe that the benefits of blogging would be worth the amount of work they would have to put into it – and, secondly, because of a fear of possible consequences. They feared that a blog's comments section could be abused or taken over by their opponents. There was also reference to the belief that comments made by Judy Dunn, the Liberal Democrat candidate in a Hartlepool by-election, on her blog caused her to lose that election.

One of the respondents to the 2007 survey was a 26-year-old female district councillor who described her blog as 'a way to connect with the electorate'. The three satisfaction descriptions that she chose agreed with Jackson's findings: helping to clarify her thinking, giving her approval and giving her support for her ideas. She also suggested that another positive benefit of her blog was that of raising her profile in the Labour party. She had started her blog in 2005 to support her parliamentary candidacy. After the election, her blog became more personal, but was transformed again into what she described as a 'councillor-blog' after her election to the city council in 2006:

> I wanted to carry on blogging after the election to show that a young, non-Blairite woman could be an active member of the Labour party and could get involved in politics, and then, after my election, could be a local councillor. At a time when there is massive disillusionment with politics and politicians, I was trying to be honest and open, allowing hostile comments and encouraging a debate.

This respondent is thus a very good example of the way in which bloggers' motivations for starting and then continuing a blog can change over time. Her desire to give a female politician's view echoes the motivations of the MP blogger Sandra Gidley, who stated that she had started her blog in order to give the female view of Parliament as well as give an insight into the local things that an MP does, which are less reported in the mainstream media (Jackson, 2008). However, echoing the fears about public servants blogging mentioned previously, the councillor blogger had got into trouble through her blogging:

> I blogged about being taken to the e-democracy conference in Budapest by DCLG [Department for Communities and Local Government], using my usual blogging 'voice' – quite flippant and irreverent. It got picked up by some Tory bloggers who objected to DCLG spending money on an international conference and then got picked up by the newspapers. I was then pilloried in my local paper over three weeks with my quotes on DCLG – which I wrote – pulled out in bold. It was dreadful – entirely of my own making in that although I had done nothing wrong I had been unwise in how I had blogged about it – but dreadful and hugely embarrassing. Unfortunately that experience is slowly turning me into one of those identikit politicians who never say anything interesting.

This is a good example of an occasion on which a newspaper journalist has found a story by paying attention to the blogosphere. Although this respondent had found that the immediacy of her blog led her to publish material that she had not fully considered in the way she might have done had she been writing for a more traditional form of publication in a newspaper, she still considered blogging to be useful for her political career. Another male respondent in 2006 found that it was actually his blogging that gave him enough confidence in himself and his own opinions to stand as a candidate for Parliament in a recent election:

> I am much more confident – and am determined to do lots of things before I exit the stage. My Dad was a brilliant writer – but very frustrated. He tried to write – in a little exercise book, that got no further than his bottom drawer. With blogging, a thought comes in – it's banged out in 'Word' and uploaded to be viewed by a potential audience of thousands, in seconds!. … That's what is great about it. It's a great way to get rid of your frustrations – and as regard to making me more confident – I stood for Parliament at the last General Election – and I cannot imagine me doing that before I discovered blogging.

Thus, the respondents were comfortable with the idea of blogging as a form of journalism, but only a minority appeared to see their own blogs in this way or attempted anything that might be described as citizen journalism. This group included both men and women, although there were fewer female bloggers than male bloggers and, as we have seen from the example of the female councillor, when women blogged about politics, they might do so because this would help them stand out as different. There also appeared to be more of a desire to use a blog to comment on and criticise local or national politicians than the mainstream media itself; thus, the idea of bloggers as a fifth estate is not particularly useful when analysing this group of bloggers. For the majority, their blogging was not journalism – it was a much more personal and internal affair, focused on their own lives and experiences rather than attempts to influence others or become embroiled in a debate about public affairs. For these respondents, their concept of blogging as a form of journalism must therefore be deduced to come from media coverage of other, A-list blogs rather than their own experiences. As one British respondent commented, distancing himself from that kind of blog: 'It's all things to all people, really – in the US it's mainly journalistic.'

Blogging as creative writing

Although around a quarter of the respondents saw blogging as a form of journalism, a similar number of respondents stated that they considered blogging to be a form of creative writing (34 in the 2006 survey and 76 in the 2007 survey). In fact, the creative writing option was the most popular option in the 2007 survey and the second-most popular option in the 2006 survey. This popularity can also be linked to the popularity of the satisfactions relating to the display and exercise of talents given in Table 3.2. The respondents were also asked why they found blogging useful and the results are given in Table 3.3.

It is obvious that the respondents closely associated blogging with the provision of an audience for their creative and intellectual work. As we saw in the quote from the would-be male politician mentioned previously, blogging is seen as a more immediate way of publishing your thoughts and opinions than writing in an exercise book and then keeping it in a drawer or attempting to persuade gate-keepers such as editors to publish them:

> I love to write and try to write amusingly. I like to have an audience. And, my blog helps me to think out and review the things that happen in my life through the medium of creative writing. It is like thinking out loud to friends, only in disguised story form. (*Female respondent*, 2007)

Table 3.3 How do you find blogging useful?

Usefulness of blogging	2006 participants (n = 48)	2007 participants (n = 120)
It brings customers for your business	7	22
It widens the audience for your intellectual work	21	39
It widens the audience for your creative work	19	62
Other reason	22	27
No usefulness	4	10

It also became obvious that the blog was not seen as an end in itself but rather as a staging post on the road to more public (and hopefully remunerative) fulfilment:

> A way to develop creative writing skills and present them to the world ... It gives me a creative outlet which is in public – if I didn't do this it would require me to get writing published, display art work in galleries etc which are all very time consuming and fraught with knock-backs and disappointment. This is a leisure activity which I can fit around a full time job and a part-time MA which provides me a space in the world to display my writing, drawing and photography and elicit feedback on it. (*Female respondent*, 2006)

We will investigate the possibilities of a blog leading to a publishing deal in more detail later.

The idea of blogging as a form of creative writing thus seems to have been a more accessible concept for these respondents than the idea of blogging as a form of journalism. While only a minority of bloggers consider themselves to be acting as journalists, far more are open to the idea that they might be publishers (Shirky, 2008: 79). The motivation of self-expression, linked to the need to articulate ideas and emotions through writing, is evidently an important element in blogging – and the desire to gain an audience for one's creative and intellectual work can also be linked to ideas of voyeurism and exhibitionism (Gurak and Antonijevic, 2008). Indeed, as blogging tools have become easier to use, it seems that self-expression and social interaction have become the dominant motivations for blogging, moving away from the earlier information gratification motivation (Trammell et al., 2006).

Thus, an investigation of the journalistic motivation suggests that this was a strong motivator for only a minority of our group of bloggers. Although they identified with the idea of blogging as a form of journalism, few saw their own blogging in such terms and the majority focused their posts on internal rather than external events. Venting and 'blowing off steam' were important factors for most respondents, but most of these types of posts were about their own lives rather than public affairs. Neither did many get involved in debates about public affairs on their blogs, although those who did tended to perceive them as stimulating rather than upsetting. However, if we widen the scope of our enquiry to include the concept of blogging as a form of creative writing, we find not only a similar high level of acceptance of this concept among our respondents but also more evidence of creative writing being part of their own personal blogging rather than merely an acceptance of the mainstream media's definition of blogging, as seems to be the case with journalism. The respondents found a great deal of satisfaction in the thought that they were displaying their creative and intellectual work through their blog and were also hopeful that the oxygen of such publicity might lead to the possibility of a wider acclaim. One hope that was frequently expressed was that their blog might lead to a publishing deal and this optimism will be further investigated and assessed in Chapter 6.

4

Beneficial blogging

I find my blog has been an excellent self-motivation tool and has helped my depression a lot. I have suffered little since starting it. As a freelance illustrator, living in a rural part of Britain, it is all too easy to slide into loneliness and the kind of mental 'bad habits' which can lead to bouts of depression. Since having my blog, and working hard to promote it, I have gradually found myself being the kind of person I would like to be. My visitors (especially US city ones) enjoy that I live in the Cotswolds, bake my own bread, grow veg, am a 'proper' (i.e. earn my living from and am published) children's illustrator living in an old cottage, and now I find that I have to keep up with the persona that they see me as on my blog – I feel as if I have a regular 'audience' and so instead of not doing things because I can't be bothered, I do them, and this makes me feel better about myself. It doesn't matter whether I blog it or not, as I am often writing blog posts in my head that never get posted – it is just a useful mental 'trick' to stop me sliding into the kind of unhappy low-self esteem kind of depression I used to be prone to. (*Female respondent*, 2007)

Now that the blogosphere has been established for over a decade, attention is turning to the question of why bloggers continue to blog once the novelty has worn off, and whether their initial motivations for blogging change over time. In 2007 Miura and Yamashita investigated the psychological and social motivations behind a group of Japanese bloggers' continued blogging. They suggested that in order to continue to blog, bloggers needed to feel that their blogging was beneficial for both their own selves and their relationships with others. Communication with readers who gave positive feedback strongly encouraged bloggers to keep posting (and we will discuss this later in this chapter), but bloggers also needed to feel that their blogging was psychologically beneficial for themselves.

> I have never known what blogging is about, except that it forms a way of exorcising the self-commentary in my head! It's a little to do with exercising some kind of wordcraft, though I wouldn't go so far as to call it a talent. It's a lot to do with taking my negativity and spinning it positive, but for my own benefit. To demonstrate to myself that there's another way of looking at things (or something more amusing to distract me from whatever's getting me down). So, a way of looking at things or a way of looking away from things ... in any event, it's more internal than external. (*Female respondent*, 2007)

As we have already seen, most of the postings in diary or journal-type blogs are focused on the personal experience or thoughts of the blogger. In their survey for the Pew Internet and American Life Project, Lenhart and Fox (2006) found that the most popular topic among blog authors was their own life and experiences. Writing about our personal experiences can help us to understand ourselves and also to deal with personal problems or conflicts. So one motivator for bloggers, and in particular for those who write journal blogs, can be a desire to deepen their understanding of themselves and to help them cope with events in their lives.

> As it gets closer to my son's birthday, I realize that I've never really blogged much about that, and I think it would be therapeutic. I still harbour guilt about the whole situation, so maybe writing about it would be a good thing. (*Scooby Snax*, 27 April 2003)

The blogger quoted above consciously perceived some of her blog postings to be part of a therapeutic experience, and expected that writing out a full account of a particularly traumatic event in her life and the feelings associated with the event would help her to fully understand and learn from that experience. Such hopes are related to both the inner spiritual journey associated with traditional diary-keeping and more modern psycho-therapeutic practices where clients are encouraged to write down their experiences in order to explore them in more depth. Writing about personal experiences can help someone understand themselves more deeply and mitigate major problems and conflicts (Miura and Yamashita, 2007). Over the past three decades, a growing body of research has demonstrated the beneficial effects that expressive writing about traumatic or stressful events can have on physical and emotional health (e.g. the early work of Pennebaker and Beall, 1986). The majority of this research has been based on the participants writing about traumatic or emotional experiences for a number of sessions, often over consecutive days, for 15–20 minutes per session, which is very reminiscent of many people's approaches to blogging. Although the participants can find the experience upsetting, they also find it valuable and meaningful (Baikie and Wilhelm, 2005). Writing about the emotions triggered by a particular event is apparently not enough on its own – the writing needs to include a description of the traumatic event itself as well as the emotions it stirred up. Such writing can be by hand or – importantly – on the computer, and can be undertaken either in clinical settings or alone, as a self-help tool.

Male and female respondents to our surveys were equally likely to suggest that their blogging had a therapeutic purpose, although female respondents were more likely to actually use the term 'therapy' about their blogging. Five female respondents explicitly described their blogging as a kind of therapy in response to an open question about how they conceived of blogging, while a male British blogger told us: 'My blogging is a positive coping mechanism for me. I find that blogging about things helps me to deal with them, emotionally.' Another male respondent stated: 'The act of blogging can act as a form of self-actualisation – re-affirming myself and my views rather than approval from others in terms of comments.' Other respondents used phrases such as 'self-exploration', 'positive coping mechanism' and 'cathartic release' to describe their blogging activity.

> Letting other people know your thoughts and dreams and reading their responses can be encouraging and inspiring. Over the years my blogging buddies have become a sort of online counselling group – whenever things get bad, or good, they're there, to cheer you on or to offer consolation. It can keep you going when times get tough and encourage you to carry on writing. Spilling your soul is sometimes therapeutic anyway! (*Female respondent*, 2007)

While most of these comments were not specific about the bloggers' mental health, several respondents did admit to using their blogging as a way of dealing with diagnosed mental health issues. One female respondent stated that her blogging offered her 'the ability to express the problems I have as a bi-polar sufferer and share and gain support'. The female respondent quoted at the beginning of this chapter, who suffered from depression, explicitly made the connection between her blogging and improved mental health, commenting that she sometimes undertook activities and then wrote about them purely for the sake of her blogging readership, but found that this activity also had a beneficial impact on her own mental well-being. However, she did not discuss her depression in detail in her blog, preferring instead to undertake activities that could positively affect her mood. She stated:

> I do try to keep my blog as impersonal as I can – if I have problems in my personal life, I keep them to myself, as I don't see my blog as being a confessional, (although as stated, I do use it as a motivational tool). I keep a 'feel good' factor going, where possible, as I see myself as 'selling' my lifestyle, with an aim to publicising my work – I am not fond of blogs that constantly go on about the blogger's personal problems and intimate experiences, so I try to remain detached in that sense.

In the blogosphere itself we often find journal bloggers using 'self-help' or therapeutic terminology when discussing their motivations for posting about certain subjects in their blogs. For example, the blogger quoted below discusses her previous computer games addiction and how her blogging helps her deal with it – whether or not she finally posts her thoughts:

> I think it helped to talk it out here, especially that nostalgia post, and other stuff I didn't post about why I quit the game. I don't really like using addiction terminology for it, but that's what fits – so, it's still one day at a time, but today's been good. (*Maewyn's Musings*, 29 September 2004)

Thus a blog can be seen as a safe place in which to explore its author's inner turmoil. However, a blog's very public nature also allows its author to communicate this exploration to like-minded people and hence to garner external support and commentary, usually from sympathetically minded readers. Six respondents to the 2006 survey (equal numbers of men and women) and eight respondents to the 2007 survey (three men and five women) agreed that they valued feedback from the readers of their blogs because it helped them come to terms with traumatic life experiences. Thus, one American blogger, whose blog focused on her battle to lose weight, described how her blog has brought a new dimension to her life:

> Why diet now? I've never had a support system like this before: I can share this stuff (stuff that I haven't shared with anybody except

my therapist) at least in part because, although you kind of know me, you don't REALLY know me: so in a way you're safe. (*Rites of Passage*, 22 July 2004)

It is striking that the idea of comparative strangers reading about one's inmost secret fears and longings – and in the case of this woman's blog also her unhappiness with her size and shape – can be described in terms of safety and security. For some bloggers, it is the very anonymity of the Internet that makes it possible to use their blogging as therapy because they find that they are more comfortable discussing their inner feelings with 'strangers'.

The internet's anonymity strikes me as rather like a confessional booth – because people reading this don't know who you are, you can be completely and totally honest with them. You can really be *you*. (*Diary of a Malcontent*, 14 January 2004)

In fact, her anonymity was so essential to this poster's blogging, that when it was breached she announced that she was closing down that blog and starting another one in order to continue with her 'therapy':

I can only hope my blog friends understand both why I am doing this, and how much it means to me to continue. This is my therapy. Just like you wouldn't want a therapist blabbing your sessions to the world at large, you understand that I similarly wouldn't want my corrupted privacy to be exploited. (*Diary of a Malcontent*, 14 January 2004)

In a similar enthusiasm for support from anonymous strangers, a respondent to the 2007 survey commented:

Getting people's opinions is a great way of helping you work through any difficult times. Sometimes the words of a stranger are easier to take on board than those of a close friend, as you don't always want the biased opinions of those who know you. You want the cold, hard truth. That's how you learn. That's how you move forward.

While most respondents were attracted to the idea that they could use their blog to discuss problems with strangers on the Internet without the fear that they would meet in real life, one male respondent in 2006 explained that he used his blogging in order to indirectly communicate his innermost feelings to his family: 'I'm not the best verbal communicator in the world. I put my feelings in the blog in the hope that my family read them, and react to them.' Using his blog, he was not forced to speak directly to family members about uncomfortable emotions, but instead could distance himself from any direct confrontation. He thus offered his family two choices: first, whether or not to read about his feelings and second the choice of either ignoring or acknowledging them, placing the onus firmly on his family to show some reaction. Gumbrecht (2004) found similar behaviour within her small sample of Stanford University bloggers – they reported occasionally preferring to communicate with friends or family through their blogging rather than by more immediate media or face to face. She points out that the limited interactivity of blogs means that bloggers can post about sensitive matters while being protected from immediate social interaction and readers can choose whether or not to respond to a post. Bloggers do not have to deal with interruptions to the flow of their storytelling when posting to a blog and therefore a blogger is able to write a post about a particular event and his or her feelings about the event without having to deal with other people's contributions or interruptions. Since bloggers have editorial control, it is even possible to remove comments added later if they are not helpful or are not what the blogger wishes to hear.

But can blogging sometimes be part of the problem rather than acting as a coping mechanism? A small minority of survey respondents (3 out of 48 responses in 2006 and 7 out of 108 responses in 2007) agreed that they sometimes felt guilty about the time they spent blogging, although others pointed out that they felt more guilt about *not* blogging and thus letting down their readers. Some posts in the blogosphere suggest (albeit light heartedly) that their writers are 'addicted' to blogging:

> The problem is, I need to do OTHER stuff rather than working on my blog. Like bathing, and eating, and maybe feeding the animals. Oh, work would be good too. Help. I am addicted. (*Atypical Female*, 6 October 2003)

This blogger explained early on in her postings that her original plan for her blog had been for it to be 'my place to vent, cry, talk about a personal illness and a beloved pet I spend a lot of time with, share joy and pain – basically let it all hang out'. In other words, she conceived of her blog as a therapeutic tool which she could use to discuss very personal and private issues. She did worry, however, that it would be very easy for a reader to google a combination of the terms she used and to find her in real life – she was not worried that she would be exposing her private matters to strangers, but was worried that the full details she planned to give would allow any interested party to track her down. However, having discussed these fears in her blog and considered closing it and opening another one in LiveJournal, where she would have much greater control over who could access her blog, she decided that her blogging *needed* to be done in public.

> One of the reasons I love my blog is that I can talk about how crazy and anal I am, and I don't have to see heads nodding in agreement. Even though I know you're doing that, and don't try to tell me you're not. I don't have to shut my eyes to go into denial, I can just close the browser window. (*Atypical Female*, 25 May 2004)

Again, we have the use of therapeutic terminology such as 'in denial' and 'anal' in the way in which a blogger discusses the self that she reveals through her blog.

Thus the possibility of using a blog as therapy is evidently a strong motivating factor for some bloggers. However, not all of the survey respondents expressed a need for therapy in their blogging or saw it as a way of garnering external support to help them deal with issues within their lives. Are there particular personality traits that might attract people to blogging or a particular sort of personality that expects blogging to provide this kind of therapeutic support?

The blogging personality

The Big Five personality inventory measures personality based on five key traits: neuroticism, extraversion, agreeableness, openness to experience and conscientiousness (Costa and McCrae, 1992, quoted in Guadagno et al., 2008). Guadagno et al. (2008) suggest that people who are high in openness to new experiences and high in neuroticism are likely to be bloggers. In particular, they suggest, women who are high in neuroticism are more likely to be bloggers compared to those who are low in neuroticism, but they found no perceptible difference for men. It may not be particularly shocking to learn that people who are interested in new experiences have been attracted to blogging in the last ten years since the whole blogging phenomenon is of a very recent origin, but the association of blogging with neuroticism may be more of a surprise, particularly if one associates blogging with the very opinionated political or news blogs that have tended to dominate media coverage of the blogosphere. Individuals who are high in neuroticism tend to be emotionally unstable, anxious, insecure, nervous and emotionally reactive. Such individuals may be attracted to blogging because they are lonely and see it as a possible way through which to form social connections with others. Those who are high in openness to new experiences tend to be imaginative and curious, prefer variety and are independent and artistic. Guadagno et al. suggest that openness to new experiences predicts maintaining a blog, and that such bloggers are likely to write about the details of their personal lives.

The work of Baker and Moore (2008) on the way in which distress motivates some people to start blogging also agrees with the above findings. In their study of a group of MySpace users, they found that those who intended to start blogging scored highly on psychological distress, self-blame and venting, and lower on social integration and satisfaction with the number of their online and face-to-face friends. They agree that studies of handwritten diary-keeping have shown that such activity can lead to significant improvements in the author's mental well-being, but point out that blogging offers the author the extra facility of peer commentary. This means that the blogger becomes open to social support and may be able to discuss subjects that they have previously been unable to communicate face to face.

Thus one of the motivating factors for people to continue to blog is the therapeutic aspects of blogging. Bloggers find that writing about a particular problem or worry that they have, even if they eventually decide not to post the final result, can be a helpful action to undertake. The idea of using writing to explore your soul or psyche is of course the same motivation behind much diary-keeping and thus this motivation can be directly linked to the journaling motivations mentioned in a previous chapter. While some use their blog to communicate about their feelings to their friends and family, others are more drawn to the anonymity offered by the Internet and the feeling that they are sharing their emotions with complete strangers, who might be able to offer objective advice, are usually supportive, and who do not know them from Adam and therefore will not be bringing difficult issues up at awkward times in real life. However, this therapeutic aspect of blogging appears to be, for most bloggers, an additional benefit of blogging that they discover once they have started and a reason to continue rather than the initial motivator to start a blog.

Letting it all out

This is not going to be one of those spiritually uplifting blogs in which I name every fetus [sic] I've ever lost and then derive comfort from the fact that I have so many little angels looking down on me from heaven. No, this is going to be an angry blog, so please spare me the lectures about my attitude ... I get plenty of opportunities to be a smiley-faced trooper in my real life. This is the only place where I get to be plain old pissed off at the universe. (*Chez Miscarriage –* 'About Me')

The above quote comes from a highly rated infertility blog written by a woman who only identified herself as *Getupgrrl*. She preferred to keep her anonymity (and that of her partner) throughout the years in which she wrote a brave and deeply felt blog about her experiences of infertility and miscarriage. This anonymity also enabled her to write with painful honesty about some very emotive issues and to defend her right – and that of other women – to undergo IVF and other infertility treatment, sometimes in trenchant tones.

As for the rules of engagement, there is only one. This is my blog. Therefore, I can say whatever the hell I want. If you don't like it – too bad. If something I say offends you, or upsets you, or annoys you – too bad. ... But feel free to channel your hate into a productive activity, like getting your own damn blog. (*Chez Miscarriage –* 'About Me')

Venting has been established for some time as a useful and cathartic component of journal writing and has been theorised to be a major benefit of blogging (Baker and Moore, 2008). As we have seen in a previous chapter, the idea of 'letting off steam' or venting was popular among the survey respondents, but more in relation to their own lives than public affairs. While they might not go as far as describing their activities as 'channelling their hate', many bloggers would agree that one of the main motivations for posting can be the need to vent rage, blow off steam about a topic that annoys or upsets them, or to just say 'whatever the hell I want'. At these times, their focus can be very much on their own needs rather than any perceived needs of their readers:

> I'm feeling sorry for any new readership right now. I just let my URL out to a few people and then I gripe for two days, LOL! But, right now I have to vent, and that's part of what a blog is for I guess. (*Atypical Female*, 30 October 2003)

Schiano et al. (2004) list the need to vent and let off steam as the first of their five main motivations for journal blogging. They comment that bloggers are surprisingly unconcerned about their privacy when undertaking these functions. Gregg (2009) has argued that it is almost a defining characteristic of academics' blogs, and particularly those of early career academics, that they offer a safe space to share the disappointments of university life. Changes in academia such as the move away from permanent tenured positions and the growth of casualisation mean that academic life is not the ivory tower it was once perceived to be and her sample of young academics used their blogs to mourn this loss and to support each other in their feelings of having been short-changed. Reed (2005) noted that, for his London bloggers, ranting was a crucial part of blogging-as-therapy and that their ranting entries tended to be longer than their other posts. He described such posts as providing an outlet for everyday frustrations – frequently related to work – which agrees with some of the responses to our surveys:

> I used to blog to moan a lot when I was a receptionist, bored out of my brain and chained to a desk. (*Female respondent*, 2007)
>
> Similarly I can moan about CILIP [The Chartered Institute of Library and Information Professionals] without having to join them, seek a journal to publish in, or write a letter to the *Times*. Anyone with similar gripes could (and sometimes has done) find my pages. (*Male respondent*, 2007)
>
> It allows me to 'vent steam' about things which matter to me. (*Male respondent*, 2006)

Others used their blog to vent their emotions about experiences and events in their personal lives:

> It started out purely as exorcism. I wanted to air my feelings about the disintegration of my abusive, alcoholic marriage, and give myself a safe space to work through my feelings and give vent to my frustrations. (*Female respondent*, 2007)

Positive feedback from readers

As we have already seen from the comparison with traditional diaries, one of the major ways in which blogs differ from diaries is that there is an expectation that the blog will be read (and possibly commented on) by others. Miura and Yamashita (2007) suggest that communication with readers who gave the blogger positive feedback was a major factor in encouraging blog authors to continue to write. They found that positive feedback from readers, for example in the form of sympathy, support or encouragement, could offer strong emotional and social support for a blogger, particularly one writing a journal-type blog, and motivate them to continue blogging. In particular, they suggest that the satisfaction of being accepted by others gives additional significance to blog writing beyond the mere act of personal diary-writing. Here, they were building on the work of researchers such as Kawaura et al. (1998), who investigated the psychological and social process of online diary-writing behaviour and suggested that, while online diarists continued to write their diaries because they enjoyed the self-disclosure afforded by these documents, they also continued because they enjoyed expressing themselves to others, and always envisioned the presence of readers when they wrote. In his study of London bloggers, Reed agreed that it was the knowledge that they had visitors – and his bloggers preferred the term visitors to that of readers – that kept the group posting regularly. Gregg's (2009) disillusioned academics found support online that helped them to develop strategies to cope with changes in their workplace.

This presence of readers is an essential factor in most bloggers' motivations for blogging. Whether they are writing for family and friends or prefer to see their readers as total strangers, the majority of bloggers are aware that they are engaged in active communication with others. What does differ across blogs, however, is who these others are perceived to be – or wanted to be.

Keeping in touch with friends

The majority of the research that has been focused on the Internet over the past decade has suggested that Internet use functions to support and strengthen social relationships and that people are increasingly using Internet-based technology to fulfil social and interpersonal needs, for example through their use of e-mail or social networking sites. For example, it is suggested that e-mail use has a beneficial effect on personal relationships and that women in particular use e-mail to communicate with family and friends and to thus maintain social ties (Boneva and Kraut, 2002). One of the questions that researchers have asked about bloggers' friendship links is whether these links reflect close offline relationships. In other words, does blogging facilitate the formation of new relationships or is it more often used to cement those bonds with family and friends that already exist?

Nardi et al. (2004a) found that many people started blogging at the urging of their friends, who were already bloggers and wanted company that they already knew in the blogosphere. Trammell et al.'s (2006) investigation of the Polish blogosphere also suggested that social interaction with real-life family and friends was an important motivation for blogging. As has been mentioned in a previous chapter, this group of Polish bloggers were very focused on personal subjects and their posts on such subjects were often vague, focused on emotions rather than on a coherent account of the event that triggered such emotions. There was little attempt at offering full explanations to their readers, but such explanations might not have been necessary if they were assuming that their readers were real-life friends and thus in fact already knowledgeable about the blogger's situation.

Many of the bloggers we surveyed also used their blogs to communicate with associates from their offline life, particularly family members living apart. For example, a woman respondent explained how she used her blog to keep in contact with friends and family: 'I can let others know what I've been up to without having to e-mail each person individually or send a round-robin e-mail.' Another stated: 'If my grown sons who live across the United States from us want to know what is going on in our lives they can read it if they wish or not.'

One of the questions in the surveys investigated how far respondents' blogging was involved with their offline lives by asking: 'Has your blogging interacted with real life in any of these ways?'

As can be seen in Tables 4.1 and 4.2, nearly half of all respondents in both surveys admitted that their blogging did interact with people they already knew in real life. In addition, a substantial minority (14 respondents in 2006, 27 respondents in 2007) agreed that they used blogging as a way of sending messages to known others, either real-life friends or e-friends. What is interesting is the number of respondents who had turned an online relationship into an offline one, and we will look at this further in the section on privacy. In comparison, a similar number of

Table 4.1 Interactions between blogging and real life, by sex, 2006 (*n* = 50)

	Men	Women	All
Meeting people in real life that you first got to know through blogging	14	11	25
Encouraging your real-life friends to blog	8	14	22
Looking at the blogs of your real-life friends	9	10	19
Other	1	5	6

Table 4.2 Interactions between blogging and real life, by sex, 2007 (*n* = 120)

	Men	Women	All
Meeting people in real life that you first got to know through blogging	18	21	39
Encouraging your real-life friends to blog	19	25	44
Looking at the blogs of your real-life friends	19	24	43
Other	5	8	13

respondents (15 in 2006 and 27 in 2007) stated that they blogged mainly for their own records. When asked why in that case she made her blog publicly accessible, one female respondent stated 'I guess initially you don't think of it as public because you don't really expect people to view your blog' while another claimed 'Because it just makes it a bit less pointless if there's more than just me reading it.'

Finding new friends

The Internet can be a tool to help people establish new friendships as close online relationships develop into offline ones as well. In comparison to the studies mentioned earlier, Ali-Hasan and Adamic (2007) investigated blog communities in the Middle East and concluded that few of the blogging interactions they studied reflected close offline relationships. The bloggers they studied reported that few of the comments they received on their blogs came from people they knew offline and they themselves made few or no comments on the blogs of people they knew in real life. There was a very small overlap between commenting interaction and offline interaction and this group of bloggers seemed relatively uninterested in the idea of maintaining existing relationships with friends and family through blogging. Instead they used their blogging to establish new relationships.

Some bloggers enjoy the idea that they are being read by complete strangers. Reed's (2005) London bloggers particularly enjoyed the fact that they could not anticipate who their readers would be and he described how their blogs could become a site for encounters. Such meetings were usually conceived of as being with strangers – indeed Reed suggested that the visits of family and friends were not welcomed by many of his bloggers because the visits of such knowledgeable social connections could lead the blogger to self-censorship, thus changing the original purpose of the blog.

For some bloggers, the possibility of making new friends is a very necessary element in their blogging. As we have seen, individuals who are high in neuroticism and nervousness might in fact blog in order to assuage loneliness or in an attempt to reach out and form social connections with others (Guadagno et al., 2008). Baker and Moore's 2008 study of MySpace users who were intending to blog found that intending bloggers were significantly more dissatisfied with the number of their real-life and online friends and also less satisfied with their current group of friends. They were therefore intending to blog in order to increase the number and improve the quality of their friends. Such dissatisfaction with their social contacts in real life was also found among the survey respondents. Eighteen out of 46 (39 per cent) in 2006 and 32 out of 104 (31 per cent) respondents in 2007 agreed that they sometimes 'preferred blogging to the company of the people I live with'.

Respondents to the surveys both found new friends and kept in touch with old ones through their blogging. And their definition of friendship included relationships with people they had never met face to face and probably never would. One woman respondent commented: 'I get satisfaction from the community that I am now part of – who I consider to be friends even if I haven't met them in person.' Another commented that she used blogging to 'meet new people', although there was no indication that she meant physical meetings.

Finding new friends online can also be easier than finding them in real life. One female respondent commented: 'I'm also a bit lazy about going out and meeting people, I also like my own company and the comfort of my own home, talking to people through blogs means I can still keep these but make new friends on my own terms.' Having a relationship 'on your own terms' also offers the possibility of staying in control of the friendship and, if necessary, keeping your distance.

As we have seen, sometimes the new online friends can become offline friends through face-to-face meetings. Even if that is not possible (or wanted) blogging contact can spill over into e-mail exchanges or exchanges away from the Internet such as through the telephone. One female respondent in her thirties stated: 'My best friend is someone I met through a friend's blog. We live in different countries but are now inseparable through IM, e-mail and phone. That is interaction huh?' Such a relationship might even embrace the old-fashioned communication channel of the postal service. In the quotation given below, the female respondent who is quoted at the beginning of the chapter explaining how her blogging has helped her depression, explains how her blogging contacts exchange more than just words:

> Through that [her blog] I have made many virtual 'friends' and colleagues, both in the same business and people who share my interests and lifestyle. Some of these bloggers have become e-mail 'penpals', and we send each other cards and little presents. This includes bloggers all over the world, not just UK ones. As I posted these gifts on my blog, calling it 'the Society of Secret Fairies' for want of a better description. Other bloggers were also posting their parcels, and we got many enquiries as to 'how to join' the SOSF. So I set up another blog in conjunction with the 2 other bloggers, (both illustrators) just for this, to organise a parcel exchange. We are sharing administrative duties and the three of us are caretakers of that blog.

She was not the only respondent who reported receiving presents from her readers. Another female blogger told us: 'I've never met any of my regular blog readers, but we regularly phone and send personal e-mail, too. They have sent gifts (bits of computer when mine breaks down, etc.) and two or three of us have supported each other through periods of unemployment and major life change. It's fairly surreal.' Another female respondent listed the mixed haul of 'goodies' that she had so far been sent by people who had read her blog: 'A haul of physical goodies: One book about Tunbridge Wells, a bag of home-grown veggies, a jar of anchovies, a pair of mittens, some maple syrup and pancake mix.'

A sense of responsibility to their readers is another factor that keeps bloggers blogging. Asked whether they agreed or disagreed with the statement 'I feel an obligation to my readers to communicate regularly', 42 out of 48 (87.5 per cent) of the respondents to the 2006 survey and 79 out of 107 (74 per cent) respondents to the 2007 survey agreed or strongly agreed. One respondent commented: 'I think worrying about disappointing other people plays a significant role in this.'

Thus, the formation and nurturing of social relationships can be a strong motivating factor in starting and continuing a blog. Unlike the therapeutic motivation, this wish to blog for friends – whether to keep old ones or to make new ones – can be a motivator to start a blog. Bloggers can be encouraged to start blogging by real-life friends and family and then use their blogs to keep in touch with them online. Such a motivator can be particularly strong if the blogger lives away from friends and family – blogging can be less formal and more spontaneous than writing e-mails or letters updating everyone on events in your life, and again the reader can choose when and even whether to log on and read the latest update, making the blog less intrusive than direct contact. Other bloggers may blog in order to increase their number of friends, looking to the blog-osphere to find like-minded new acquaintances, possibly when they are in short supply nearer to home. Such friendships can develop into offline relationships or, if distance is a problem, into e-mail, telephone or even postal communication. Whether or not the relationship develops offline, bloggers are appreciative of the support and friendship they can receive from their readers. Perhaps this can be best summed up by the description of blogging given by a divorced college lecturer somewhere in North Carolina as 'A public forum where someone non-judgmental is theoretically listening' (*Diary of a Malcontent*, 14 January 2004).

5

Do privacy concerns impact on blogging motivations?

Given the very public nature of blogging, we need to explore how concerns about privacy might impact on the motivations of would-be and continuing bloggers. This is particularly problematic for journal bloggers, with their focus on their own lives and experiences. Over half of the respondents to both surveys reported having experienced problems with family, friends or employers as a result of their blogging. How do they try to ensure that they do not reveal too much online – and what do they judge 'too much' to be? How anonymous can a blog be, and how anonymous do bloggers want their blogs to be? For many, the attraction of blogging is the idea that strangers can read and respond to their posts, and we have seen that some chose to blog in order to find new friends online. For these bloggers, using mechanisms such as restricting their readership in order to protect their privacy would be counter-productive.

> The inspiration for my blog comes from many of the people I know in real life – there is always the danger that they may (a) find my blog; (b) recognise certain events or people described and (c) they may get very cross! But writers need copy and copy comes often from daily life experience.
>
> (*Female respondent,* 2007)

To a great extent, journal bloggers appear to rely on pen-names and the vastness of the blogosphere in contrast to the very limited interest that their blogs might hold for anyone stumbling upon them accidentally (Nardi et al., 2004). Trying to find a specific person's blog is very difficult if you do not know the title of the blog and they do not advertise their full name in their blogging. However, once hit upon, many blogs offer a great deal of personal information, sufficient to identify individuals, and real-life confrontations over what has been said on a blog have led to anything from momentary discomfiture to legal difficulties. Thirty per cent of the respondents to Technorati's survey on the State of the Blogosphere (2009) reported that they found it important to conceal their identity when blogging. The main motivator here was concern for family and friends, but 19 per cent were worried about the reaction of employers. Similarly, Viégas (2005) reported that 36 per cent of her mainly American sample had found themselves in trouble of some kind as a result of their blogging. She also found, unsurprisingly, that the more personal the material published, the more likely it was that the blogger would experience problems. She suggested that bloggers experience their blogs as an intimate, secluded space and are tempted into spontaneity by the ease of posting, whilst the reality is that they have little control over who might read their blogs – or how such readers might react to personal information.

Secret from friends and family

> Nobody knows I do this ... My family don't know and my friends don't know ... I'm not sure why I feel the need to keep it from them ... maybe it has something to do with the fact that most of what I write about is them. (*By a Woman*, 30 October 2002)

We have already seen when discussing blogs-as-diaries that some blog providers such as LiveJournal offer bloggers the opportunity to limit access to both their actual posts and the commenting facility. Thus LiveJournal bloggers can choose to open access to their blogs only to select family and friends. As a female respondent to the 2007 survey explained: 'My personal blog is friends-locked on LiveJournal to stop prospective employers etc. reading more personal entries'. Thus one way to deal with the privacy issue is for bloggers to restrict their readership. Such an approach will only work, however, when the main motivation for keeping a blog is to keep in contact with real-life friends and family or to use the blog as a personal and private diary. Restricting access would not be of use to a blogger who is motivated to blog in order to make new connections online or who wishes to reach an unknown audience with information or opinion.

In direct contrast to those who choose LiveJournal because it helps them restrict their readership to offline friends and family, other bloggers are trying hard to keep their blog secret *from* their closest associates – and such reticence is often because the blogger wants to write *about* their family and friends, and not necessarily in a complimentary way. The quote at the beginning of this section comes from an early post in a blog started in 2002 by a British mother in her thirties. She made it clear at the start of her blog that she was writing for her own purposes and saw her blog as a combination of a diary and a therapeutic tool rather than for a readership. Despite these motivations, however, she did not attempt to limit her readership in any way, relying on the fact that the blogosphere is a big place to keep her anonymous. In fact, she remarked that, luckily, her husband was 'not technically minded and will probably never find this site, so I can write what I like about him'. Her posts were for herself, not for others, and in fact she was very aware of how some of these posts might hurt or upset her friends and family if they ever read them. Another blogger's need for anonymity resulted in an intermittent style to her postings since she had to close down her blog whenever someone else entered the room. Her posts sometimes included warnings that she would not be able to write for a while because members of the family would be around. It is reminiscent of the apocryphal stories of Jane Austen writing away on her little pieces of paper and hiding them whenever someone else enter the room. Chandler (1998) mentions the lack of hard copy as a reassuring aspect of personal homepages and, in practice, a physical diary may be harder to hide than the existence of an electronic one. Interestingly, the motivations of the blogger of *By a Woman* started to change very early on in her blogging and she quickly grew to appreciate her online readership – recording her excitement when she received an e-mail from a reader only a few days after she started blogging: 'can't believe people may actually be reading my drivel'. Two years after starting the blog she recorded her 10,000th visitor and noted 'I'm sure that although I didn't start this with actual real-life readers in mind I would have given up long ago without you guys to keep me company'. Thus although she had started her blog as a private diary, this blogger quickly found that she soon became enraptured by the feedback she received – but it was feedback from strangers that she particularly sought, not from people who knew her in real life.

Reed (2005) also found that his London bloggers were eager to attract strangers to their blog, but not as happy to find friends reading it. Sometimes this development led to self-censorship and the blog lost its original purpose. As a female respondent to our 2006 survey explained:

> I would prefer to remain as anonymous as possible because otherwise I would find myself self-censoring. As I have already done when my partner started to read it. While I don't use my blog to complain about other people in my life, I still want the freedom to be able to say whatever I want without worrying about the effect it may have if that person reads it.

Another woman respondent reported changing her blogging behaviour as a result of finding out that her ex-husband read her blog:

> One of the reasons it's become less personal is because my ex-husband reads it, and I do feel that much of what I write is none of his business – particularly since he does attempt to use it against me. However, taking it down would feel like admitting defeat!

Her ex-husband had attempted to use her blog posts as evidence against her in a custody battle over their children. However, she reported that, against his expectations, the excerpts from her blog used as evidence in court actually worked in her favour and she was granted custody.

Thus finding that a specific person is reading their blog might cause a blogger to change the way they post or even in extreme cases to stop blogging entirely. The blog of a student in Bloomington, Indiana, reported how she was 'weirded out' to be informed by her boyfriend that his mother now read her blog. She worried about how the mother had reacted to the intimate descriptions of the two young students' love-making and decided that more censorship was now needed. A blogger in Belgium reported on the shock she received when an acquaintance in her office commented 'I loved the write-up of me and my wife's a great fan of yours'. She had no recollection of mentioning him in her blog at all and reflected bitterly that 'Belgium is *too* small'. Her boyfriend suggested that on his next visit to London he should approach random strangers and offer praise of their blog in order to completely panic them. However, this blogger, who writes a blog entitled *My Boyfriend is a Twat*, clearly got over any feelings of embarrassment or worries about her privacy since in 2007 her blog was published in book form by The Friday Project under her real-life name – Zoe McCarthy, thus outing her to all and sundry. (The phenomenon of blogs being turned into so-called 'blooks' is discussed in more detail in a later section.)

Some bloggers address the privacy problem by writing more than one blog. Around half of the respondents to the surveys (27 out of 48 responses to this question in 2006 and 47 out of 104 in 2007) admitted that they had more than one on-going blog, with different blogs having different purposes and sometimes different readerships. Similarly, Technorati's *State of the Blogosphere 2009* found that the average respondent had three or more blogs. For example, one female respondent had a blog under her real name and another under a pseudonym where she felt that she could whine and moan about her life more. Other bloggers' motivations for multiple blogs might be related to the subject matter. A male respondent stated: 'I have a LiveJournal which is Friends Only for very personal posts and my [other blog URL] for stuff anyone in the world can read.' One female American blogger explained:

> I've considered starting a second blog just to lay out all these adventures in their ripe, juicy glory and honestly the more I stew on it the more the idea appeals to me. While I love this blog and keeping in touch with my friends and acquaintances is precious to me – I think that even I feel a touch apprehensive ... at laying it all out in all its delicious sybarite glory. Plus, I have the occasional child peeking at this blog, and I disdain restricting my posts to friends only. (*Kalkail's Journal*, 7 August 2004)

Wood (2008) agrees that anonymity on the Internet can be particularly helpful in the context of blogs about sex and suggests that women can be freed by such anonymity to have discussions including intimate details about their sex lives or their own bodies, which they would not be able to undertake with friends in real life. However, blogging about such personal subjects can often only be done if the blogger is convinced that his or her anonymity is secured. One female respondent in 2006 told us:

> A previous now defunct blog got me into big trouble at work. The content was fairly sexual ... it was discovered at work. I'm a staff nurse. My employer said she had strived for 30 years to abolish the idea that nurses were sex objects and I had destroyed that in a few words.

Secret from employers

'I am worried with the current trends of employers firing people for making comments on their blog regarding who they work for, I feel that we all have a right to free speech in any context.' (*Female respondent*, 2006)

As we can see from the story about the nurse, concerns about privacy can also be related to employment. There are basically two issues associated with blogging and work. One is the wider issue of the use of an employer's facilities for non-work-related Internet use. A 2005 survey for an American body, the Society for Human Resource Management, found that 20 per cent of its members had fired employees on these grounds (Hopkins, 2005). The other issue is content. There have been quite a few high-profile cases in recent years concerning bloggers being dismissed for blogging at or about their employment. For example, in January 2005 a Waterstone's employee was dismissed by the book chain for blogging about his employment at their store in Edinburgh. In the United States an airline attendant who called herself *Queen of the Sky* was dismissed by Delta Air Lines for 'inappropriate images' on her blog that showed her in her airline uniform. Again, this woman, Ellen Simonetti, has gone on to publish a book about her experiences and to attempt to forge a career as a media commentator. There is even a word for such dismissals – according to UrbanDictionary.com, to be 'dooced' is to lose your job for something you wrote on your blog. Heather B. Armstrong, who writes a blog called *dooce.com*, was one of the first bloggers in the United States to be sacked from her job for making derogatory remarks about her fellow workers in her blog. One British survey respondent, who uses the blog name *The English Courtesan* and uses her blog to advertise her rates and specialities as a call-girl, stated: 'The rise of "doocing" is a real concern for courtesans and anyone else who writes about their sexual exploits – La Petite Anglaise and Abby Lee (*Girl With A One Track Mind*) were just two recent media exposes.' More recently, the sex-blogger and author Belle de Jour, whose blog, *Diary of a London Call Girl,* was successfully published as a book and later made into a television series, outed herself in November 2009 as Dr Brooke Magnanti of the Bristol Initiative for Research of Child Health. Magnanti stated that she was revealing her identity on her own terms before an ex-boyfriend could do it for her. Like Magnanti, Armstrong and the other two bloggers mentioned by this respondent are now published authors, suggesting that once one's anonymity has been lost, it may be possible to capitalise upon any concomitant infamy by forging a new career in the media, if only for a limited amount of time.

Also in 2009 the anonymous author of the blog *NightJack*, who had been awarded the Orwell Prize for political writing in April of that year, was outed by a journalist from *The Times* as Detective Constable Richard Horton of the Lancashire Constabulary (Gibb, 2009). Despite Horton seeking a legal injunction to stop the newspaper revealing his name,

Mr Justice Eady ruled that the blogger could have no reasonable expectation of anonymity because 'blogging is essentially a public rather than a private activity'. This was a landmark decision that may well have an impact on many other bloggers who rely on keeping their anonymity while writing about their work, friends, family or other aspects of their lives and their opinions, and specifically places blogging in the public rather than the private sphere. The *NightJack* blog offered its readers an insight into frontline policing, but also included Horton's strong views on social and political issues. Some of the most popular sections included anecdotes about cases on which the detective constable had worked. Although Horton changed details such as the names of people and places, once his identity was known it became possible for the actual cases to be identified. Horton was issued with a written warning by his superiors and his blog was deleted.

Guadagno et al. (2008) suggest a notion of 'relative anonymity' with reference to the way in which bloggers may reveal more information on their blogs than they realize. They suggest that people who communicate online experience a reduced awareness of the other individuals who might be reading their words, and point out that not only have bloggers been fired because they have blogged about their jobs, but other stories in the media give examples of bloggers who have confessed online to crimes they have committed or affairs they have conducted with seemingly little awareness of who might be reading such admissions. The cases mentioned include a murder in 2007 where a 17-year-old boy stabbed to death his 15-year-old girlfriend's mother. Both teenagers had blogged about their feelings and activities before and after the murder on their MySpace blogs, including references in the girl's blog to 'doing the laundry' for her boyfriend – apparently a reference to washing his bloody clothes (Healy, 2007).

More amusingly, in February 2009 *The Times* newspaper investigated a 'confession craze' said to be sweeping the Internet whereby bloggers were encouraged to confess '25 random things' about themselves. Those who had already succumbed to the urge were said to include MP Tom Harris, the former transport minister, who admitted to having stolen a roll of Sellotape from a newsagent as a child and John Prescott, the former deputy Labour leader, who admitted crying at the film *Billy Elliot*, which he has been to see six times (Woods, 2009). The majority of these lists were created using the 'notes' blogging section of the Facebook site. Commenting on the phenomenon in *The Times* article, professor of psychology Mark Griffiths made the point that, because it is a non-threatening and dis-inhibiting medium, the Internet encourages people to reveal things that they would never reveal in face-to-face conversation or, it must be assumed, in an interview with a journalist.

Our surveyed bloggers were definitely concerned about the impact of their blogging on present or future employment opportunities. They were also aware that future employers might search the Internet for information about them before deciding to offer them employment or even an interview, and several expressed worries about postings they had made in the early days of their blog before they became better informed about the Internet's archiving and search facilities. Even if they subsequently deleted these posts, or even the entire blog itself, this is no guarantee that a future employer might not be able to search out damning evidence using facilities such as the Wayback Machine, which allows you to 'surf the Web as it was' from 1996 to the current day (*http://web.archive.org/collections/web.html*). As one male respondent commented in 2006: 'the damage is done and there is now no going back'.

Many of the survey respondents were anxious to keep their private and professional lives apart and worried about employers or work colleagues reading their blog. As one male respondent put it: 'There are certain people for whom I work who I would not really want to see my blog, simply from the point of view that it puts forward a side of me that differs slightly from my professional front'. Another stated that moving to a new job had made him limit what he wrote in his blog: 'Since moving in to a new job my posting has almost ceased as I try to get a handle on what's allowed or not. ... It's not so much retribution from above, but from colleagues who may not understand the nature of some of the comments I make (i.e. devil's advocate)'. Others were very aware that their blog could get them into serious legal trouble:

> 'Writing about people or companies that I have worked for I shroud them in anonymity, so that my friends would know who I'm writing about, but not a casual passer-by to my blog. This is to avoid litigation or suchlike, stories of which have become more prominent in the press recently' (*Male respondent*, 2007).

This response demonstrates the way in which bloggers can be aware of, and write for, more than one audience at a time – here the blogger writes in a way that assumes that his friends will understand far more of the background or implications of his posts than casual readers would pick up.

For some respondents, their blogging had already impacted negatively on their employment. In the 2006 survey, two of the respondents reported being warned not to blog at or about work and one admitted that she had been sacked after bitching about work colleagues on her blog. A male respondent to the 2007 survey who worked as a freelance journalist even claimed harassment by the American government, stating:

> I have no doubt what I write is held against me by my peers, my editors, people in the defense/industrial/entertainment complex. I have lost work because of my blog. I've also had what could be called light stalking (from mostly women trying to find out where my house is) and surveillance activity (government, I assume).

It should be noted that some bloggers have no issues about being identified and, indeed, see their blog as part of their employment. A good example of this type of blogger is the religious minister who blogs as part of his or her outreach to their community. Our surveys included several ministers who used blogs as part of their ministry and indeed one major motivator for a substantial minority of our respondents could be encapsulated under the heading 'God', including one respondent who described himself as a member of an online evangelistic gaming ministry. Another respondent was a Methodist minister who served as a chaplain for Swansea University and therefore used blogging as a way of communicating with students. He gave a full name and contact details on his blog plus a pencil drawing of himself rather than a photograph. He commented: 'As a minister, a large part of my job is about communication. Blogging is one way of widening the reach of what I believe to be an important message. I think that's the main reason I do it.'

Other bloggers who revealed personal data about themselves did so because the blog linked to their job. For example, some respondents used their blog to market either themselves or their services, and thus needed to make their contact details at least available to interested readers. Others used their blog to discuss professional issues. For example, one American male respondent who worked as a lawyer focused his blog mainly on legal issues. His comments on such issues carried much more weight with readers because he clearly identified himself as a qualified lawyer with full details of his background and links to his company's website.

Does a concern with privacy result in a limiting of the amount of information given about the blogger in his or her blog? When selecting blogs for our studies we found that we had to discard many otherwise suitable bloggers because they did not offer an e-mail address or any other way of contacting them on their blog. This was particularly true of women's blogs. In contrast, we found that women (and gay men) were slightly more likely to put a photograph of themselves on their blog. In some cases this was done even while the blogger withheld other personal detail such as their name, suggesting that they did not mind being recognised by people who already knew them, but were wary of being identified by strangers.

There is a gender dimension to concerns about privacy. In general, women in both the United Kingdom and the United States tend to be more concerned about the negative aspects of the Internet (Media literacy audit, 2006; Fallows, 2005). In both surveys more women than men said that they had concerns about privacy, although some men also had such concerns (in 2006 16 women and 12 men admitted to having concerns about privacy out of 47 responses to this question while in 2007 25 women and 18 men were worried out of 100 responses). These concerns mostly related to being identified, whether by employers, colleagues, friends or family. Concerns ranged from the mild 'some people at work might be a bit snarky about it if they knew I was writing it' (*Male respondent*, 2006) to the more alarming 'I've also had stalkers, people threaten me physically or to "out" me as my real-life persona' (*Female respondent*, 2006). Gay bloggers in particular mentioned concerns about family members or co-workers discovering their blogs.

Others worried about strangers identifying them from their blogs. Nardi et al. (2004) suggest that many blogs contain sufficient information to identify individuals even if they try to remain anonymous. One female respondent reported: 'I do worry that my home and my habits can be identified from the blog – one reader (who lives nearby) worked out the building I live in'. Another stated: 'A recent and unhealthy case of cyber-stalking merely reinforced to me how important it is to keep anonymity online.' Two male respondents told us about being recognised by readers from photographs on their blog – one in his home town and one in the lounge of an international airport. It should be noted that while the two female respondents found the possibility of identification worrying these two male respondents made no such comments.

Our survey respondents also provided a good amount of information about the steps they took to protect their own and others' privacy, including of course blogging anonymously. For example:

> I do not use my real name on my blog because I am concerned that people could find the blog by searching for me on a search engine. I also do not publish pictures of my children or wider family to respect their privacy ... I am careful what I disclose on my blog about myself or anyone I know and I will often change minor details to disguise who I am writing about if needed. Everything I write about is true, but only a few people know that it is me that writes it. (*Female respondent*, 2006)

However, although many of the bloggers surveyed stated that they took steps to hide their identities and location and the identities of families and friends mentioned in the blog, such care was not consistent. In our 2006 sample, one-quarter of the women and half of the men gave their full name on their blog. The overall figure of 37.5 per cent is comparable with the figure of 31.4 per cent in Herring et al.'s (2004a) sample of 203 English-language blogs. Viégas (2005) states that 55 per cent of her sample of 486 mainly American bloggers gave their real names, but she does not specify that these were 'full' names. In addition, 63 per cent of her sample was male. Photographs were given on the blog by 35.4 per cent of the 2006 sample (17 bloggers), which is higher than the 17.5 per cent in Herring's sample, possibly because technological changes made it easier for people to upload photographs to their blog in the intervening years.

Anonymity may carry a penalty in relation to popular success as it means losing the opportunity to transfer social and cultural capital from the blogger's real life identity to the blog. Thus women's greater concerns about privacy on the Internet may be one of the reasons why their blogs are generally less highly rated than men's – an issue we will return to in a later chapter.

So do concerns about privacy and a desire to retain anonymity impact on the motivations of bloggers? The evidence suggests that such concerns can at least alter a blogger's behaviour. Once they are aware that someone they know offline is reading their blog, then a blogger may self-censor their opinions or the way in which they describe certain events or feelings, aware of the possible reactions of their offline acquaintance, either online in the comments section of the blog, or face-to-face. Such self-censorship is usually perceived as a negative consequence of having real-life acquaintances reading the blog – I have not come across a blogger who expressed any appreciation for having to introduce a more objective viewpoint in their personal writings, although as we have seen, a comment from a stranger challenging their opinions can be appreciated as refreshing and thought-provoking. Bloggers can also be very aware of possible offline consequences of reckless blogging, whether these are with friends and family or current or even future employers.

There is also a concern, particularly among women bloggers and some gay bloggers, about being identified by strangers because of details on the blog. This leads to bloggers consciously hiding the identities of themselves and others that they blog about although, as we have seen, such an approach is rarely consistent, and a trawl through the archives of most journal blogs can provide a determined would-be stalker or vengeful ex with a good amount of information about a blogger's location, employment and family. Several of our survey respondents mentioned problems arising from their blogging, either with friends and family or, less frequently, with strangers.

If a blogger is motivated primarily by a desire to keep an online diary for therapeutic reasons or to keep in contact with offline family and friends, then privacy worries can be solved by merely utilising the restrictions offered by providers such as LiveJournal. However, if a blogger wishes to communicate freely online and has started a blog in order to contact others with similar interests or to persuade others with their opinions and knowledge, then such restrictions are not useful and that blogger needs to come to terms with the possibility of losing their anonymity online. As we have seen, some bloggers have chosen to make their personal details available online from the beginning – sometimes because their motivation for blogging (whether commercial or something more spiritual) requires their reader to know who the blogger is. Posts about religion or law may be more convincing when the reader is aware of the qualifications of the blogger to make such statements. Other bloggers are 'outed', usually because of the controversial nature of their posts: criticisms of employers or salacious sex stories. On occasion, such bloggers are able to use their consequent notoriety to change career and establish themselves in the media.

The majority of bloggers, however, do not have one nice neat motivation to help them decide whether or not to restrict their readership. As we have seen throughout this book, most bloggers are motivated to blog by a mix of reasons – and such motivations can change as their blogging career progresses. Some bloggers attempt to deal with this problem by having more than one blog – around half of our survey respondents (27 out of 48 respondents in 2006 and 47 out of 104 in 2007) had more than one blog, some of which were of the restricted type for the sake of privacy. Others dealt with the problem by attempting to monitor their output for too much personal information and by changing or fudging details when necessary. Whatever their particular approach to the problem of privacy, and whatever trouble that they had got into because of their blogging, what is most interesting is that the bloggers carried on blogging.

6

The money motive

Technorati's *State of the Blogosphere 2009* distinguished four types of bloggers among its survey respondents. By far the largest group was the hobbyists, who made up 72 per cent of respondents. These bloggers blogged for fun and had no expectations or intentions of making money through their blogging. The second group, the part-timers – who made up 15 per cent of respondents – blogged, at least partly, to supplement their income. The third and fourth groups were blogging professionally, either as part of their own business or organisation (the self-employed, 9 per cent) or as employees of another (the professionals, 4 per cent) (Technorati, 2009).

Since I first started my investigations into bloggers' motivations in 2003, I have become aware of a growing financial motivation in the blogosphere. Would-be bloggers can now buy books entitled *Start Your Own Blogging Business* and *ProBlogger: Secrets for Blogging Your Way to a Six Figure Income* (a blook based on a popular blog). Blogging now offers most bloggers the opportunity to raise at least a small amount of money from their blog through hosting advertising, although, of course, not all wish to go down this route. For a more select group, as we will see, blogging can lead to substantial financial gains, through advertising sales, the publication of the blog as a book or the sale of the blog itself.

A growing awareness of the financial rewards of blogging has grown in the blogosphere over the last decade. In my first analysis of women bloggers' motivations, I found no mention at all of monetary reward for blogging. However, in the responses to the 2006 survey, a small group of our sampled bloggers mentioned the money-raising potential of blogging. For example, one male respondent stated:

> I blog for two reasons; firstly it amuses me and secondly it provides an income stream through giving me an easy and structured way to

generate content which I have monetised [sic]. (*Male respondent*, 2006)

Others said that blogging was useful for its indirect financial rewards: it brought customers to their business – it was 'a route to obtaining clients for the design business' – and that their clients often read the blog and so it could be used to communicate with them.

In addition, a number of the surveyed bloggers regarded blogging as 'an adjunct to work', and for a minority (six women and two men out of 48 respondents), blogging appeared to be more central to their livelihoods. They indicated that blogging was useful to them because it brought customers to their business, that it was financially useful and that they regarded it as an actual or potential source of income. This group was not characterised by any superficially obvious patterns of age, educational attainment, length of time spent blogging or number of hours spent blogging in the previous week. Nor was there any regularity in the age of their blogs or their sophistication, the number of blogrings they subscribed to or the numbers of outward links or images per 1,000 words. However, a high proportion of the group worked from home (four of the women and one of the men) and two of these women claimed to be blogging on a full-time basis (35 hours a week). One of these was a graphic artist who used her blog to showcase her work, which included her current projects of a graphic novel and some cartoon strips. Blogging had already brought her several commissions and also recognition in her field. The other described herself as a semi-professional blogger and again used the blog to showcase her freelance journalism.

Both of these women, although describing themselves as full-time bloggers, were, in fact, using their blogs to promote and showcase their offline work. However, the later (2007) survey included two respondents who had actually managed to turn their blogging into real careers – one was a British respondent who worked as a freelance blogger, setting up blogs about West End shows and for individual actors. As she put it herself: 'instead of blogging to moan about my lack of a decent job, I blog for money!' Similarly, an American woman respondent reported that her blog of film criticism, originally set up for her friend's amusement, was now syndicated across three newspapers in her home state.

In the 2007 survey, a slightly higher proportion – 22 respondents (nine men and 13 women) out of the 120 surveyed – agreed that blogging brought customers to their business. Again, this revenue generation motivation was particularly strong among women respondents who were looking for ways in which to generate income as an alternative to full-time employment outside the home. As one British woman respondent willingly admitted when asked why she blogged: 'I hope to eventually make enough money from my blog to support my family, I see it as the beginnings of an online business.' Another stated: 'I started the blog as a way of promoting my online business, enhancing online word-of-mouth marketing for my business and developing my brand.' Her business sold home furnishings and *objets d'art* online and the blog described how she tracked these objects down, described, with photographs, how she furnished her own home and, latterly, how she and her family were moving to the United States but hoping to continue to run the business from there.

Blogs can be effective marketing and communication tools for small businesses, and these possibilities have been highlighted by the business press for some years. In 2005, both *Time* and *Business Week* ran special issues devoted to blogging, while *Fortune* put blogs as number one in its '10 Tech Trends to Watch for' (Hill, 2005). However, using blogging as a marketing tool can be time-consuming for lone workers and small businesses. In his investigation into the attitudes and experience of small business bloggers using blogs as a marketing and communication tool, Hill (2005) suggested that blogs were better used for relationship building with the business's clients rather than direct sales. Only one respondent to his survey in 2005 was making any money through the sale of advertising and most found that the main constraint that acted upon their use of the blog was a lack of time. From the reports of my survey in 2007, the situation may have changed slightly, with more bloggers at least expecting to raise a small amount of money from hosting advertising on their blogs and many others hoping that their blogging will lead to greater things. A British respondent who worked as a children's book illustrator reported that she showcased her work and sold associated greetings cards through her blog. Although the illustrator found that her blog attracted enquiries from potential clients for her artwork, another respondent – and a very different sort of 'home-worker' – was using her blog to attract clients. Describing herself as an English Courtesan, she stated that many of her clients came to her through her blog, which offered details about her rates and specialisms, and that many of her fellow sex-workers also used blogs as a form of marketing.

Pro-blog commentators recommend that companies encourage their staff to keep blogs in order to give a human face to the company and to build up a positive feel around its products (Xifra and Huertas, 2008).

A corporate blog can be used to establish dialogue between the company and its target market and to create new, more enduring relationships with a customer base that is becoming less interested in brand messages delivered by traditional media (Singh et al., 2008). For example, in their recent book aimed at businesses on how to exploit social media, Newson, Houghton and Patten (2009) recommend blogging as an inexpensive way of raising the profile of both the company and the blogger, pointing out that blogging can be much more efficient at communicating with large numbers of people than mass mailshots or e-mail, where much corporate material is now stopped by spam filters. Blogging can be particularly beneficial for companies whose potential clients are web-savvy. They can be used for market research to target particular segments of a market and to build relationships with customers (Singh et al., 2008). Gillmor (2006: 23), however, warns that it is essential for companies to establish a corporate policy about blogging, about what can and cannot be said on a corporate blog. He recommends offering an RSS feed on the blog so that the company's message has a chance to reach all those interested in hearing it. Subscribing to an RSS or news aggregator means that each of the new posts from the blogs you are interested in following will automatically appear on your computer. Thus it becomes possible for infrequent bloggers to serve their established readership without the readers becoming frustrated by continually having to check for new posts.

However, although the majority of commentators agree that blogs can offer companies a powerful new tool with which to establish dialogue with customers, there are doubts about whether the average corporate blog is currently being used efficiently or effectively. In her work on corporate blogs, Forbes (2009) found that the majority of the sample blog posts she analysed were non-interactive and half of the blog postings did not even generate comments. The importance of both adequate resourcing and 'buying in' to the idea of corporate blogging by both employees and management cannot be stressed enough. It is not enough for a company to set up a blog or to assign responsibility for it to certain members of staff. Corporate blog postings need to be frequent, responsive and interesting enough for their customers to want to read them, and this needs commitment from the corporate bloggers. Without such commitment, a corporate blog cannot succeed in all its objectives. This is reminiscent of the problems faced by mainstream media sources when their journalists are not open to blogging (previously mentioned in Chapter 3) and similar problems faced by educationalists attempting to use blogs as part of their teaching (see Chapter 7). The need for commitment and investment by the (forced) bloggers themselves is paramount for the success of such enterprises.

Advertising

Of course, as well as promoting blogger's talents, blogs can also make money through carrying advertising or offering subscriptions. As one American male respondent in the 2007 survey pointed out bluntly:

> Money from advertising is a very large reason that people stay blogging once they become popular, because it's very easy to make small or even large sums of money through advertising. Ask people who run popular blogs and some will even admit that it's the only reason they do it, or at least a large part. It's hard to say no to a simple buck.

There is a growing interest in blog advertising on the part of media agencies. Blogs can deliver extremely focused audiences in terms of interest and demographics. The Internet offers a serious rival for advertising income to mainstream newspapers and magazines, and blogs are particularly useful for establishing and exploiting niche audiences that may be too small or geographically scattered to be addressed by a traditional print publication. A blog on the subject of parenting a child with special needs or lawn green bowling will attract readers with similar experiences or interests, thus offering product manufacturers easy access to such niche markets. Many bloggers have signed up to companies such as Google Adwords or Blogads, which place advertising on a website roughly based on the topic of the page. Lopez (2009) points out that the so-called 'mommy bloggers' were targeted by advertisers at the 2006 BlogHer conference in which a new session was offered entitled '$$$ Generation' and the BlogHer Ad Network was launched with an initial test group of parent bloggers. The readers of such mommy blogs are educated, website-loyal, married women who tend to make purchases on behalf of their whole families – perfect for advertisers. However, Lopez suggests that there has been a fierce backlash in the blogosphere against mothers who host such advertising on their blogs, with suggestions that it might compromise the editorial integrity of their blogs and even that, as mothers, they should somehow be above such money-making endeavours.

While the majority of bloggers will not make their fortune through such revenue generation, most find that it provides a small income, possibly enough to cover their blogging expenses. A male blogger from the United States, whose blog specialised in advice about genealogical research, admitted: 'A successful blogger can earn a small income by hosting advertisements. While not enough to support a family, it may be enough to pay for one's genealogical research fees, subscriptions, etc. I do consider blogging a part-time job.' By the 2007 survey, bloggers were becoming confident enough about the advertising possibilities of their blog to attempt to reach advertisers directly rather than making use of the agencies: one male respondent's blog carried a section offering the possibility of running a banner advertisement at the top of his blog for a month with the guarantee that no other advertising would be accepted during this time. He charged £200 a month for this privilege.

Such bloggers may have been inspired by press coverage of highly successful bloggers who now make enough money from the advertising sold on their blog to devote themselves to it full time. The sole income of the Armstrong family, for example, now comes from advertising space sold on Heather B. Armstrong's very popular blog *http://www.dooce. com*. Armstrong started writing her blog in February 2001 and, by October 2005, had attracted enough advertising to enable her husband to leave his job to support her on the technical and business aspects of the blog. A feature article about her in the *San Francisco Chronicle* in July 2008 suggested that at that time her blog received 5–6 million page views a month.

Armstrong's success has also attracted the attention of the print publishing world. In 2008, she took a step into the bookshops by editing *Things I Learned About my Dad*, a collection of short essays taken from popular parenting bloggers such as *Finslippy* and *Laid Off Dad*, and, in 2009, she produced *It Sucked and Then I Cried: How I Had a Baby, a Breakdown, and a Much Needed Margarita*, a book focused on her experiences of post-natal depression, which were, of course, also documented in her blog.

Advertising on Dooce is sold through Federated Media Publishing, which handles the advertising for several other bloggers, including those mentioned previously as contributors to *Things I Learned About my Dad*.

Advertising is not the only source of potential income for bloggers. Other bloggers have raised money by selling merchandise, writing product reviews or even selling their successful blogs to larger media companies. A name frequently mentioned in the business press in connection with blogging and revenue generation is Weblogs Inc. Set up by Jason Calacanis and Brian Alvey in 2003, Weblogs Inc. was an umbrella company aimed at creating niche business blogs, with individual bloggers as partners with Weblogs Inc. Money was made through advertising revenue and the blogs concerned included some very popular ones, mainly in the area of technology, such as *Engadget*. In 2005, AOL bought Weblogs Inc. for a reported $25 million (Gillmor, 2006: 153; Newson et al., 2009: 45). Weblogs Inc. currently offers 90 blogs, including popular and respected blogs *Engadget, Joystiq* and *Autoblog*.

There is even the possibility of raising money through direct requests for donations on your blog. For example, Joshua Micah Marshall of the political blog *Talking Points Memo* asked his readers to help him travel to New Hampshire to cover the presidential primary in January 2004. They raised more than $4,000 (Gillmor, 2006: 155). One enterprising blogger from the original 2003 study, now based in Berlin, carries a button on her blog entitled 'Support my DIY Masters' requesting donations via Paypal.

Another innovative use of blogs to market a product was reported in *The Times* of 5 July 2009. Christian Braun, owner of an unusual house in Baron's Court, London, had launched a blog in order to sell his house. The house, formerly owned by an artist and with strikingly large windows, had failed to attract a buyer in the time that Braun had it with a local estate agent and so he set up a blog (*http://rememberthewindow.com*) devoted to the house and the history of the surrounding area in the hope that more interest could be raised this way. After two months, he was able to tell the *Times* reporter that, while the estate agent had provided only two or three viewings since the previous autumn, the blog had already attracted seven viewings and an offer of an exchange from an artist in Mallorca (Brooke, 2009).

However, although financial profit certainly seems to be a growing motivation for blogging, not all respondents were so positive about the potential for money-making through blogging. Two respondents, both male, explicitly stated that they were not looking to make money from their blogging and one of these admitted that he had started blogging 'to see if I could drive traffic and earn money ... now it's for pleasure and fun. Money doesn't matter'. Interestingly, in the 2007 survey, one American male respondent felt that his strongly worded views of US government policy that he put forward on his blog had actually led to a loss of work from the defence industry. He also considered that blogging was a threat to his career as a journalist: 'Sadly I feel my work abilities (writer, reporter, photo-journalist) are going to go the way of the dinosaur. Note the rise in cheap digital stock imagery, blogging, "citizen" journalist submissions to network and cable TV, websites, publications, etc. (all for free, mind you).'

Blooks

While the majority of our respondents were hopeful that their blogs would bring them a little money through advertising sales, a smaller group of respondents hoped for a different sort of financial recompense. They were hoping to be discovered by a publisher or agent through their blogging and to thereby establish a career as an author. In the United Kingdom, these bloggers' hopes were stimulated by the publicity that surrounded the publication of books such as Belle de Jour's *Diary of a London Call Girl* and, more recently, *Wife in the North*. The outing of Dr Brooke Magnanti as the blogger Belle de Jour has already been mentioned. Her blog, supposedly the confessions of a London call girl, was first noted by *The Guardian* in 2003. A book based on the blog was published by Orion Books in the United Kingdom and the United States and, in September 2007, a television serialisation, based on the book, starring former *Dr Who* assistant Billie Piper was shown in the United Kingdom. It has since been shown in the United States and a second series started in the United Kingdom in September 2008.

The publication of *Wife in the North* is of more recent origin. At the end of 2006, Judith O'Reilly, heavily pregnant and with two small children, moved from London to live in a small cottage in Northumberland in the north of England. The family was in pursuit of her husband's childhood dream to live in such a rural vastness. However, her husband did not actually move with the family. He retained his job in London, lived there for most of the time and became an infrequent visitor to his family. In the meantime, O'Reilly struggled to cope with the isolation, the complete change in her lifestyle and the exhausting job of looking after her small family and at the same time organising the complete refurbishment of the cottage they had bought (Grice, 2008). A professional journalist cut off from the London media world in which she had once worked, O'Reilly turned to blogging to express her thoughts and emotions. Her blog was officially launched in January 2007 and, within ten days, she had a book contract. Viking Penguin offered an advance of £70,000 and the book was published in July 2008, with an initial print run of 35,000 copies. In the same month, it was Radio 4's Book of the Week. The book has been acclaimed by reviewers as both funny and very moving. It is a best-seller in the United Kingdom and has been recently published in the United States.

Wife in the North and *Belle de Jour* are examples, albeit very successful examples, of blooks: blogs that have been transformed into books. And many of our respondents felt that they too had a blook in them. For example, one female respondent explained: 'I have aspirations to write a book about the food industry and I believe that writing the blog is a tool to (1) exercise my writing muscles and developing a voice; (2) distinguish or create a unique voice; (3) offer me opportunities for credibility and to be viewed as a subject matter expert.'

What precisely is a blook? Although the term can also refer to an online book published via a blog, the generally accepted meaning is the idea of a printed book based on blog postings. It is generally accepted that the first blook was *User Interface Design for Programmers*, by Joel Spolsky, published in June 2001 and based on his blog *Joel on Software*. However, the term blook appears to have been invented the following year, when journalist and blogger Jeff Jarvis suggested it as the title for the printed book of a fellow blogger's postings. Of course, the publication of books based on serialised newspaper or magazine articles is nothing new. During the Victorian period, works by authors such as Charles Dickens and Elizabeth Gaskell were originally published in parts or as magazine serials, thus enabling publishers to spread the costs of publication and widening the market for their works to include those who could not afford an entire book in one purchase (Feather, 2005). It should be remembered that Helen Fielding's *Bridget Jones' Diary* started as a column in *The Independent* and with its short, chronologically ordered entries might very well have been a blog if it had been written a few years later.

The advent of the Internet has offered the opportunity to move such part publication online, with one example being Stephen King's *The Plant*, although problems arise connected with payment when the publication remains online and it should be noted that King did not complete his experiment with *The Plant* (Palko, 2007). Other authors and their publishers, however, can now experiment with using their blogs to publicise their printed works, posting digital content – either parts of their books or sometimes even the entire book, perhaps for a limited period – on their blogs or elsewhere on publishers' websites in order to publicise it directly to their core readership (Nowell, 2009).

Blooks even have their own prize. In 2006, the Blooker Prize was inaugurated by print-on-demand publisher Lulu.com, whose publications list features many blooks. The founder of Lulu, Bob Young, has stated that while conventional publishers want 100 books that would each sell a million copies, he wants a million books that will each sell 100 (Cohen, 2007). The definition of blook that Lulu.com used for the prize was a book derived from blog content. The competition was open to any English-language blook, published by either a conventional publishing house or a self-publishing company. The first Blooker Prize competition for blooks published in 2005 was won by a cookery blook: *Julie and Julia: 365 Days, 524 Recipes, 1 Tiny Apartment Kitchen* by US blogger Julie Powell. The blook is based on Powell's 2004 blog and is the story of her attempts to cook all 524 recipes in Julia Child's *Mastering the Art of French Cooking, Volume 1* in a year. In 2009, the film of the blook – the flook? – was released starring Meryl Streep as Julia Child and Amy Adams as Julie Powell and offering, as an extra stimulant to would-be bloggers, the possibility that one day their own lives, as documented in their blog and then augmented by a screen-writer such as Nora Ephron, would become a Hollywood movie.

Given that the Blooker prize is open to any blook published in English within a particular year, I decided to further investigate the blook phenomenon by analysing the entrants to the 2006 prize. In particular, I wanted to investigate the publishers of such blooks, the background of the authors, the success of the blooks and whether their authors continued to blog after their blook was published. What type of author and subject combination was likely to produce a successful blook?

The 2006 prize had three prizes: for fiction, non-fiction and comics. In addition, one of these winners was acclaimed as the overall winner. Judges for the 2006 prize included the blogger Arianna Huffington, the previous year's winner Julie Powell and the British journalist Nick Cohen. Only printed, bound books were eligible, the blooks had to be written in English and significant amounts of the printed material had to have been developed online. The complete details of 53 of the entrants were sourced from the Blooker Prize blog (*http://lulublookerprize.typepad.com*) (there was no definitive list given on the blog and the related prize website has been closed). The prize winners for the 2006 Blooker award were *Mom's Cancer* by Brian Fies (comics winner: a category that attracted very few entrants), *The Doorbells of Florence* by Andrew Losowsky (fiction winner) and *My War: Killing Time in Iraq* by Colby Buzzell (the non-fiction winner and the overall winner).

Of the 53 entrants, 37 were written by male authors, 14 were by female authors and there were two blooks written by groups of mixed-sex authors. The majority of the blooks fell into the non-fiction category with 35 entrants, whereas there were 15 fiction entrants and only three comic blooks. Interestingly, all but two of the fiction authors were male. The most popular topics in the non-fiction category were relationships (five blooks by five female authors) and war (five blooks, four by male authors and a historical analysis of Christmas in the trenches during the First World War by a mixed-sex team). So far, so stereotypical. There were also three blooks on religion (all male authors) and two each in the categories of health and business advice. Other categories covered included living abroad, cookery, parenting and politics.

Of the 53 blooks, 28 were self-published entrants. Perhaps unsurprisingly, 20 of these were associated with Lulu.com, the sponsors of the prize. Lulu. com does not claim to be a publisher. On its website, the company prefers to describe itself as 'a digital marketplace that eliminates the traditional entry barriers to publishing' (*http://www.lulu.com/uk*). Lulu.com claims that, in 2007, it published more than 98,000 new titles globally. Books are printed on demand and 'creators', rather than authors, receive 80 per cent of the income. Six of the self-published blooks made it into the short lists for the Blooker Prizes: two in the comics section and three for the fiction prize. One of these was the eventual winner of the fiction prize: *The Doorbells of Florence* by Andrew Losowsky. In March 2007, *The Sunday Times* ran an article on the Blooker Prize that included an interview with Losowsky, at that time one of the shortlisted authors (White, 2007). It explained how his blook of short stories was inspired by a trip to Florence, where he found himself wandering around the city alone and started photographing the different designs of doorbells in the old city. The article went on to ask whether such blooks might bring fresh life to the publishing industry, allowing publishers to access new talent and also discover ready-made markets in the hordes of readers already reading an author's blog. However, it finished by warning against the expectation of literary riches through this route into publishing. When asked how many books he had sold so far, Losowsky good-naturedly admitted that he had sold only 17 at the time of the interview, not including copies bought by him. This was, of course, before Losowsky won the Blooker Prize for Best Fiction. *The Doorbells of Florence* was re-published by Chronicle Books in March 2009, and it is to be presumed that the publisher expected higher sales because of the publicity surrounding the award of the fiction prize – it certainly brought coverage of the blook in *The Guardian*, which used photographs and text from the blook as an interactive article in its online newspaper in May 2009. Losowsky, by the way, is by no means an amateur in the field of writing. His website reveals him to be a freelance British journalist and writer now living in the United States who has published articles in *The Guardian, The Times, The Independent* and *The Wall Street Journal*. He has also been associated with several other books, some self-published and some, such as *The Time Out Guide to Barcelona*, from more mainstream publishers. This Blooker winner was no neophyte in the publishing world, and I began to wonder how many other Blooker authors would turn out to be professional writers seizing blooks as just another way to access their audience rather than completely new voices entering the publishing business.

Still focusing on the self-published blooks, I investigated how many of them were for sale via Amazon and, if they were selling there, whether any of them had a high sales ranking. It must be remembered that the research was undertaken a year after the Blooker Prize and, therefore, nearly two years after many of the blooks were published. Thus, high rankings and sales should not be expected, although Lulu.com specifically states on its website that its books are available through Amazon and, because it is a print-on-demand company, there should be no issues with regard to a book being out of print. Twenty of the 28 self-published blooks were available through Amazon, although, of these, nine were listed but were given no ranking, implying few or no sales through the website. The highest ranked self-published blook, with a ranking in the 400,000s in July 2008, was *Surviving Paradise*, written by Michael C. Perkins and based on his blog of the same name. Another Lulu.com publication, the blook offers advice on how to surf and swim safely in Hawaii and seems rather a departure from the usual subject matter for Perkins, whose other books, co-written with his brother, are concerned with the economics of the Internet and investment. Not surprisingly, when you consider that the brothers are the founders of the high-technology business journal *Red Herring*.

Perkins has published one other book with a self-publishing company, iUniverse. This is a co-authored novel about life and death in Silicon Valley. It seems, therefore, that Perkins is another established author who is using self-publishing and the blogosphere to expand his range and test the market for alternative writing projects rather than a particularly new voice discovered through his blogging.

Which were the most successful blooks entered for the Blooker Prize? Again, using Amazon, and with the repeated warning that many of the blooks had already been in print for two years, the blooks that had sales rankings up to 100,000 in July 2008 were identified.

The most successful blook actually had a ranking under 5000. It was *My Secret: A PostSecret Book* by Frank Warren. Warren has published four blooks in a similar vein all based on his blog *PostSecret*. The blog is billed as an experiment in community art and invites people to send in anonymous postcards that make art out of their innermost secrets. *My Secret* is the second blook based around the blog and focuses on postcards submitted by school and college students. Warren now undertakes speaking tours at universities across the United States, billed as PostSecret events.

None of the ten most successful blooks were self-published. The publishers included HarperCollins, Penguin, Simon & Schuster and Random House. Only two were fiction, with the rest being non-fiction and six of the ten were on the Blooker short list, including the overall winner. Three of the authors were female, the rest were male. Two of the blooks were focused on business advice. Again, one of the authors, Seth Godin, is the author of nine other books, several of which have been bestsellers, featuring in the *New York Times* business bestsellers list. However, both of the business blook authors are obviously committed bloggers as well, posting their business advice on a frequent, usually daily, basis and Godin, in particular, appears to be a prolific blogger, who started his current blog in January 2002. Of all the blogs linked to the Blooker Prize, Godin's was the earliest established and one of the highest ranked as far as Technorati rankings were concerned. Thirty-one of the Blooker-nominated blogs were ranked by Technorati, with Godin's blog ranked the second highest (15th in September 2008). The highest-ranking blog represented in the Blooker Prize was *The Daily Kos*, which offers US political analysis from a liberal perspective. This is a team-written blog and one of its writers co-wrote the Blooker shortlisted blook *Crashing the Gate*, again one of the top ten sellers according to Amazon.

The key thinking behind blooks is that well-received blogs, with high readership numbers, should bring their market with them when they are turned into books. To a certain extent, the blooks submitted for the Blooker Prize bear this out. Many of the better-selling blooks, ranked high on Amazon, also carry high rankings on Technorati, demonstrating a readership that is eager to read the thoughts of these authors both in print and online. Good examples of this include the cookery blook *Vegan Lunchbox* and the erotic memoir *Girl with a One-Track Mind*. *Vegan Lunchbox* is a particularly good example of a true blook. Established as a blog in September 2005 by the stay-at-home-mom Jennifer McKann, *Vegan Lunchbox* started to win blogging awards almost immediately: winning PETA's Proggy Award for Blog of the Year in 2005, the 2006 VegWebby Award for 'Best Family Blog' from *VegNews* magazine and the 6th Annual Bloggy Award for Best Food Blog. In turn, these awards attracted the attention of publishers and the blook was published in 2006 by Little S Press, with a second edition coming out in August 2008.

Girl with a One-Track Mind is a Belle de Jour-alike. Again written by a British author, the blook takes a year's worth of entries from Abby Lee's blog, which focuses on frank writing about her sex life. Abby Lee is the pen-name of Zoe Margolis, a camera operator in the film industry who has since carved out a career for herself as a media commentator (Williams, 2006). The blook was published by an imprint of Random House in both the United Kingdom and the United States, although in the United States the blook was given the title of *Diary of a Sex Fiend* suggesting, according to the author, that Americans needed things spelled out for them a little more!

With these two cases, good Technorati rankings transferred into high sales. Another blook that sold reasonably well was based on the blog *Random Acts of Reality*, written by Tom Reynolds, an Emergency Medical Technician working for the London Ambulance Service. His blog is consistently highly ranked by blog-tracking directories and has been named Medgadget Best Medical Blog and Best Literary Medical Blog. The associated blook is entitled *Blood, Sweat and Tea* and was published by The Friday Project, an independent publisher founded in London in 2004. This publisher's main stated aim was to source material for printed books from the Internet – for example, in November 2005, the company published an anthology of British bloggers, including excerpts from Tom Reynolds' blog. The Friday Project had a confident start in the publishing world and, in 2006, was able to hire Scott Pack, ex-buying manager from the book chain Waterstones, as commercial director. In May 2007, its managing director Clare Christian was awarded UK Young Publisher of the Year at the Nibbie Awards. However, after a bad Christmas, the company was forced into administration early in 2008, with HarperCollins buying some of its assets – Reynolds' second blook, *More Blood, More Sweat and Another Cup of Tea* was published in June 2009 under The Friday Project imprint of HarperCollins. Criticism of The Friday Project in the blogosphere suggested that although it had managed to get several of its titles featured on the *Richard and Judy Book Group* television programme in the United Kingdom, the company had not had the resources to sign up enough bloggers with general appeal, such as O'Reilly or Belle de Jour, both of whom were published by mainstream publishers, and instead were forced to turn to well-written blogs focusing on more narrow interests, which did not always translate into high enough book sales to sustain the company's ambitious expansion plans.

In other words, a popular blog does not necessarily translate into a popular book, and an Internet readership will not necessarily become a book-purchasing market. The blogging style: short, chronologically ordered entries, does not always easily translate into a book, and some of the more popular blooks mentioned previously have been rewritten to remove this formulation. Very topical writing becomes less topical when it is published months later. The transformation of a blog into a blook usually also removes the comments of readers and the way in which the blogger interacts with his or her readership. In some cases, this is the heart of the blog and by removing this interaction the blog becomes less interesting or readable. Yes, some popular blogs become best-selling blooks, but that appears to be more to do with the writing skill of the blogger than with the blogging format. As we have seen, many of the bloggers shortlisted for the Blooker Prize turned out to be successful authors in other formats and it is possible that their book would have been published anyway if they had taken the idea directly to a publisher. Their commitment to blogging may also be debatable. At least four of the blogs entered for the 2006 Blooker Prize had been closed down by summer 2008 and several others were being added to much less frequently, and mainly with details about the book and where to buy it. Yes, bloggers such as Seth Godin and Tom Reynolds continue to blog as frequently as ever, but for others, the blogging experience seemed to finish once their blog had been turned into print, whatever the success of the blook.

This is not to say that the blook phenomenon has not unearthed some successful books that would probably never have seen the light of day if they had not started as blogs. The overall winner of the 2006 Blooker Prize was *My War: Killing Time in Iraq* by Colby Buzzell. In his article detailing his experiences as a judge for the prize, Cohen had only praise for Buzzell's book, arguing that it would never have been written if blogging had not been invented and that Buzzell had been given confidence in his own abilities because of the on-going praise he received from his readership (Cohen, 2007).

Colby Buzzell had no interest in a career as an author before his blog became popular. He was a soldier. He was not hoping that his blog would become so popular that it would attract the attention of publishers: he was more concerned about not catching the attention of his superiors, who ordered him to close down his blog when it was eventually discovered. His blook has been tremendously popular and Buzzell has gone on to write articles for magazines such as *Esquire*. On leaving the army, he used the GI Bill to enrol for a photography course at his local college. Unfortunately, he was not able to keep up the blogging as frequently, but one of the main reasons for this must be that, in May 2008, he was recalled for deployment in the Middle East.

I originally chose to investigate the blook phenomenon because of the reported hopes of many of my surveyed bloggers that their blog would soon lead to contract negotiations with a publisher. As we saw in an earlier chapter, the concept of blogging as a form of creative writing was popular among respondents to both surveys, and several stated that they were hoping that their blogging would lead to greater things. Such hopes may be overly optimistic. The blook is not a guaranteed way for publishers to source new best-selling authors and blooks are not challenging the way in which the publishing industry operates. The demise of The Friday Project suggests that a total reliance on material sourced from the Internet is not – as yet – a winning formula for the publishing industry. A highly ranked blog is not necessarily a guarantor of a best-selling book, although some authors have managed to cross over. However, many of the successful blooks discussed here were written by professional writers and it seems that blogs and blooks are to some extent being used by already established authors to experiment with other genres. Once published, there is no guarantee that the author will continue to blog with the same vigour as before or on topics other than the promotion of their new book. For some blooks, the readership of the blog has successfully been transferred to the associated book and even on to the associated film or television series. Having said all this, however, just occasionally – as with Colby Buzzell – blooks are a way in which a brand-new writing voice can catch the attention of the public.

7

Blogs as tools

One reason that someone might write a blog is because of its usefulness. Blogs can be used to store information, for individuals or organisations, and they can be used to transform that collection of information into useful knowledge. Early categorisations of blogs often distinguished between filter blogs, journal blogs and what they called knowledge blogs (k-logs), which tended to be the smallest group. For example, Herring et al. found that over 70 per cent of blogs in their sample were written by individuals on largely personal themes, with only 12.6 per cent being filter blogs and 3 per cent k-logs (2004b). Others distinguished between interaction through blogging – driven by the need for self-expression, life documenting and commenting – and content gathering, which is driven by the motivations of forum participation, commenting and *information seeking* (Chun-Yao et al., 2007, my italics). Such a distinction might be comparable to distinctions between journal and filter blogging, although, as has already been noted, most bloggers blog from a mix of motivations.

This chapter investigates the motivations of bloggers who produce information-related blogs, whether these blogs are for themselves, their work or for some other organisation, for example for educational purposes. In particular, it reflects on the importance of personal motivation in the success of such blogs – as we have already noted in the case of blogs associated with mainstream media, a blog will not succeed if the person charged with blogging does not have a personal commitment to the project.

Blogs as tools for teaching and learning

The use of all kinds of online educational technologies has been enabled by the advent of Web 2.0 and the use of such technologies is on the rise in both schools and higher education establishments. This is in reaction to a variety of factors, including the increasing number of distance or open-learning students and the familiarity and ease that the younger generation of students is assumed to have with the Internet. The way in which the Internet can act as a means to deliver content and provide students with access to information has been seized on with enthusiasm by many in education. It is argued that young people are used to commenting on the contributions of their friends on Facebook and other social networking sites and therefore will be open to using Internet tools such as blogs as educational tools. However, some studies suggest that students still primarily see the Internet as a tool for communicative and social software uses rather than a means for accessing educational information (Selwyn, 2008 – and it is interesting that in this study blogging was classified as a purely communicative tool rather than associated with teaching and learning).

There are good arguments for the use of blogs in teaching and learning both in schools and in further and higher education. Blogs can be used to enable interaction between individual classmates or between a class and its teacher or to offer peer assessment and feedback opportunities (Duffy and Bruns, 2006). Blogs can support learning in a number of ways: they can be used by students and tutors to gather and exchange online resources – particularly useful for disciplines where printed materials quickly become out of date; comments can be made on students' blogs by both their peers and the tutor; and they can be used to establish communities, particularly among geographically distant students. One of the first major blogging initiatives in higher education was established at Harvard University in 2002. The Harvard weblogs project was the product of a conference at the Berkman Center in November 2002 entitled 'What is Harvard's Digital Identity?' and aimed to promote lifelong learning and a community based around Harvard (Williams and Jacobs, 2004).

Blogs are deemed to be particularly useful for subjects that have traditionally used some kind of reflective journal keeping as a way in which students can reflect on their progress, for example foreign language classes or teacher training. The informality of blogging, in contrast to the formal language demands of assignments, can encourage more experimentation on the part of the student and the blog can serve as an online portfolio of their work. It offers a place for writing practice, but also the possibility of a responsive audience through the written comments of tutor and classmates. Huffaker (2005) contends that blogs can promote literacy through the use of storytelling in classrooms and because of their ease of use they are suitable for all ages and both genders. Blogs can also assist individuals to develop their own writing voice, which may discourage plagiarism and encourage more interaction in classroom discussions (Oravec, 2003).

Teachers can also use a blog in order to communicate with students outside class time. Through their blog they can direct students to appropriate resources on the Internet, offer more information than is possible within the confines of a scheduled class and write about subjects in a more personal or informal voice. This type of blog could be used by the teacher over a number of years in order to build up resources and teaching materials, which can be made accessible to the students even after the teaching time has finished. A male respondent to the 2007 survey who lectures at a British university reported:

> I sometimes feel guilty blogging at work but I see it as intellectual and self-development, and most of my recent academic output seems to have come from initial blog entries, so I really see it as a tool. In fact, I introduced several students to blogging with such good results it's now compulsory on one course I teach.

It is interesting that he has made blogging compulsory since this touches on one of the key debates related to the use of blogging in education – whether or not it should be optional or compulsory. As will be seen below, some of the proponents of the use of blogs as an educational tool suggest that such blogging must be on a voluntary basis if students are to make the best use of such a flexible tool.

One of the main early uses of blogs in higher education has been to offer distance-learning students a way of communicating informally with both their peers and their tutors. Dickey (2004) argues that blogs provide new strategies for bridging the feelings of frustration and isolation suffered by some distance-learners and that the informality of blogs allows students to 'vent' and express their feelings as well as to respond to their assignments. Blogs can also be used by students as storage systems for useful information – links, their own notes, drafts of essays. Kerawalla et al. (2009) investigated postgraduates' use of blogs within an Open University course and suggested that there were six factors that influenced these students' blogging: perceptions of, and a need for, an audience; perceptions of, and a need for, a community; the utility of and need for comments; the presentational style of the blog content; the technological context; and the pedagogical content of the course. For these postgraduate students, unlike the students in the male respondent's class mentioned above, blogging was not a compulsory part of the course. The course materials suggested some blogging activities, but students were free to use their blog in any way that they wished. Overall, Kerawalla et al. found five types of blogging behaviour among these students: blogging avoidance; resource network building; support network building; self-sufficient blogging; and anxious, self-conscious blogging to complete the course activities in the mistaken belief that blogging was compulsory (Kerawalla et al., 2008). Those students who did use their blog were generally appreciative of the way in which their blog was owned by themselves and was a place for their own learning and thinking. It should also be noted that some of the students enjoyed having a place where they could communicate with and vent their frustrations to their peers and appreciated the informality of the blog. Not all students appreciated the networking opportunities offered by a blog, however – a few did not blog at all and chose not to engage with the course community through their blog but instead used it purely as a store for their own notes and materials. Kerawalla and her team note that such behaviours challenge the popular assumption that blogs are primarily a communication tool. Overall, they found that the majority of the students found blogging to be helpful in supporting their learning, but that there was not one way in which the blogs were used. This very flexibility of blogging can mean that it can cause problems for educators who wish to introduce blogging into the classroom.

The introduction of blogging into the curriculum does not necessarily guarantee positive outcomes. Problems associated with using blogs as learning tools include minimal or haphazard contributions to their blogs by students; students writing a bare minimum in their blogs in order to achieve a minimal pass; students' difficulties in understanding the rationale behind blogging; and limited or no communication between students in their blogs (as cited in Kerawalla et al., 2008). Many of these issues are not exclusive to blogging or indeed Internet-based educational tools, but instead will be familiar to most teachers and university lecturers who have dealt with any classroom-based activity. The reluctance of some students either to share good ideas or information or to criticise, and perhaps undermine, someone else's efforts, and the knowledge that even an apparently informal discussion may be making an impression on an assessor, even if not formally assessed itself, can make many students unhappy or unwilling to contribute to class discussions and projects.

De Almeida Soares (2008) reported on a class blog that she set up with nine pre-Intermediate EFL students in Brazil with the aim of fostering a sense of community and establishing a collaborative discussion space where students might reflect in more depth, in writing, about themes developed in class. She hoped that the students would be able to develop critical reading and writing skills by commenting on and correcting each others' written work. However, she discovered that the students were unwilling to contribute or respond to comments on the blog, although they were happy to read it in class. Her conclusions were that she had been naïve to think that just because her students were computer literate they would take to blogging eagerly and that she needed to make time in class for them to contribute to the blog rather than expect them to blog at home. Similarly, the MBA students surveyed by Williams and Jacobs (2004) at the Queensland University of Technology found blogs an effective aid for teaching and learning but felt that they needed greater direction at the beginning of the course in how to blog and what they could expect to get out of it.

Such issues with using blogs in teaching led Krause (2005) to state three basic rules for the use of blogs in teaching in an article for *The Chronicle of Higher Education*. First, he felt it to be important to acknowledge that students may not necessarily want to blog. Second, he contended that blogs do not help writers interact – he found that his students barely acknowledged each others' postings and felt that a discussion forum or e-mail list would offer more possibilities for such interaction. Third, he suggested that blogs work best for publishing texts that are more or less finished. In contrast to Krause, Duffy and Bruns (2006) argue that discussion forums are not necessarily better than blogs because blogs enable individual voices to have a specific space of their own whereas discussion forums are community spaces where individual voices can be lost.

The use of blogs as educational tools is therefore still a subject for debate and, again, the main criterion for success appears to be commitment. Blogs can be very flexible tools – Oravec describes them as a 'malleable and fluid medium' (2003: 225). Teachers can find blogs to be useful as an information store for themselves and their students or as a tool with which to communicate more informally with students outside class or others in the profession. Students can find blogs similarly helpful in providing communication and support between peers, particularly when they are geographically distant; as an information store; as a way of communicating informally with tutors; and as an online portfolio of their work, where drafts might be commented on by tutors or other students. However, this very flexibility of blogs can also bring problems. Students may be confused or uneasy about the rationale behind an educational blog; may be worried about being judged by others; may simply not wish to blog; or may undertake the least amount of blogging necessary to pass that class. To at least tackle this last point, blogging should probably be used as an optional tool rather than a compulsory or assessed part of a course. It is evident from the research already undertaken that blogging can be a very useful educational tool, both as a form of information store and a support and communication mechanism, for students and teachers who wish to use it, but as usual such uses can not be forced on the unwilling blogger.

Academic blogs

Part of my 2007 research project involved the establishment of a related blog. When contacting potential survey respondents I directed them towards my blog to read about and comment on the project. This had two main benefits: first, it established my credentials as a researcher with some sort of history in the area of media and communication. The blog included links to some of my previous articles and research projects and also to my university webpage. Second, it established me as a member of the blogosphere, thus validating my interest in the respondents' blogging habits and demonstrating a personal understanding of the pleasures and pains of blogging. Thus, I was positioned not merely as a researcher peering into the blogosphere from the outside, but part of it – a fellow blogger. What I had not expected was that several of my respondents linked to my research blog in their own blogs, commenting on the fact that they had been asked to contribute to my research and even encouraging their readers to get in contact with me to become involved. Later on in the project I posted some preliminary findings from the survey on the blog and was gratified when these findings were discussed and debated by some of my readers, and not merely those who had responded to the survey but others who were interested in the research. Thus I found that the blog, which I had started mainly to validate my research, became another rich source of data collection and also enabled me to discuss my research directly with the blogging community rather than only with other academics. Murthy (2008) identifies this rich interactive potential in research blogs, arguing that they allow the researcher to engage in collaborative ethnography where the community can become invested in the researchers' work through consultation and critique, which is what I found happening. Like Mortensen and Walker, Murthy suggests that such blogging can be conceptualised as part of the Habermassian 'public sphere' in which communication has the potential to become more democritised. Similarly, Erwins (2005) states that the link-focused nature of blogs allows for greater cross-fertilisation of ideas and facilitates conversations over time and space with one's peers and the research community at large.

Thus, blogs can enable a researcher's communication with both academic peers and the community they are researching. Additionally, of course – as this book demonstrates – blogs can be rich sources of data themselves. Blogs offer low-cost and instantaneous techniques for collecting substantial amounts of data (Hookway, 2008). They can help a researcher to access geographically distant populations and, because anonymous bloggers can be relatively unselfconscious about what they write, blogs can be used by researchers similarly to the way in which diaries have been used in historical or anthropological research. Indeed, Hookway argues that blogs can offer better resources than diaries since they are easier to find and access, being publicly available online and thus more available than unsolicited diaries, but also avoiding the problems related to diaries written for a particular research project. However, he warns that even unsolicited blogs will have been written by a self-aware author, self-selecting episodes to present him or herself to their readership in a particular light and that researchers need to take such impression management into account.

One of the key figures in discussions about academic research blogs is Jill Walker, an early academic blogger in Norway who celebrated the liberating and democratic dialogue to be found in academic blogging in the article 'Blogging thoughts: Personal publication as an online research tool' written with her colleague Torrill Mortensen in 2002. She became a blogger in 2000 and found it to be an important tool for her research, enabling her to develop a writing voice and a network of researchers interested in the same topics. She contends that blogging helped her to earn her PhD and find her first job (Walker, 2006). In a similar way, the male lecturer who responded to the 2007 survey reported that his blog had led to 'invitations to write articles, helped seal the deal on a book contract, and to test ideas for it'.

However, a later article written in 2006 reported Walker's growing ambivalence towards her blog now that she is established within the academic hierarchical system and aware that her blog is read by her students, peers and management. Gregg (2009) follows up on Walker's article by suggesting that a notable generation gap exists between those academics who blog from secure positions within the profession and PhD and junior faculty bloggers with more marginal employment status. According to Gregg, the first group tends to blog because of a belief in the necessary transparency and accountability to the public of academic work while the second group looks to the blogosphere for support and company.

Erwins (2005) warns would-be academic bloggers about potential implications for job security, suggesting that academic search committees may be put off by the very existence of a blog, concerned about what a new appointee *might* blog about after he or she is hired. This was reflected in the experience of the 2007 respondent:

> Another time I admitted that I was not particularly well, though quite obtusely. A student read it and while, on this occasion, it had a positive outcome (there was a lot more open discussion of stress and its effects) I did worry it might cause issues in future job applications. It could also have gone the other way.
>
> I want to write a long post about mental health to stimulate debate, but don't feel able to because (ironically) of the very stigmas I want to challenge.

Walker defines three sorts of research blog: one written by public intellectuals, or those who wish to establish themselves as such; research logs; and pseudonymous blogs regarding academic life. She notes that academic blogs that are written under their author's real name tend to be focused on traditional content and research whereas pseudonymous bloggers write about the other parts of an academic life, including the process of research and teaching, but not the content. Gregg (2009) suggests that these three types: 1. emphasise the identity of the researcher; 2. emphasise the research and 3. emphasise the workplace culture. Similar to Walker, Newson et al.'s (2009) discussion of legal blogs distinguishes between pure law blogs written by academics; law firm blogs, which discuss and provide information in the legal areas in which the firm practises; and personal law blogs with a main focus on the person employed in the legal area and their feelings rather than the law.

A good example of such a personal law blog was *Anonymous lawyer* (*http://anonymouslawyer.blogspot.com/*). This satirical blog was written in the persona of a bad-tempered hiring partner at a prestigious New York firm and a blook of the same name was later published and submitted for the 2007 Blooker award (see Chapter 6 for further discussion of the blook phenomenon). Kerr (2006), who is a legal blogger himself, argues that blogs do not provide a good platform for serious legal scholarship because the blog format forces the reader to focus on the latest posting rather than the most important thoughts, which may have been written much earlier. He does, however, agree that blogging can be useful in disseminating scholarship and offering quick commentary on new developments. He points out that in 2006 the circulation of the *Harvard Law Review* was 8,000 per issue while the most popular legal blog, *The Volokh Conspiracy*, received 25,000 visits per day. He also agrees that blogs are useful for establishing legal professionals as public intellectuals, and in a way that circumvents traditional gatekeepers such as newspaper editors.

Blogs can thus be useful to academic researchers in several ways. They offer the possibility of establishing more informal connections with their peers and their research community. They may also provide primary data for researchers in a similar way to diaries or research journals. PhD students and junior faculty members can use blogs to sustain supportive online relationships, to develop their own writing voice and to establish their expertise in a particular field. Older academics can use their blog to disseminate scholarship and establish themselves as public intellectuals. However, the very fact that so many academic blogs are pseudonymous demonstrates some of the problems associated with academic blogging. Concerns regarding the impact of blog postings on future or current careers, students or managers mean that academic blogs dealing with the realities of academic life as opposed to research are usually hidden behind pen names or very carefully written with a clear eye on the wider audience.

Information gathering

As information professionals, librarians and information managers have been quick to seize upon the potential of blogs as both personal and organisational tools.

Blogs can be used by libraries for both internal and external knowledge management. Writing on the subject of 'Why information professionals cannot afford to ignore weblogs' Pedley (2005) explains how libraries can use blogs to keep users informed about library news, services and resources. He suggests that blogs are more useful in this regard than newsletters or even e-newsletters, which are published periodically in comparison with the constantly updated blog, and are usually tied to a few writers or editors while blogs can offer news from many viewpoints. More personally, librarians can use blogs to keep abreast of their field and to be aware of what other information professionals are debating and discussing.

Blogs with the main aim of the conveyance of professional information can also offer the opportunity for the blogger to express his or her own opinions about this information (Bar-Ilan, 2005). Starting discussions with readers or providing details about their personal lives are usually of secondary importance to this group of bloggers, although the content and format of the blogs might drift over time (ibid.). For example, one of my original group of women bloggers, a Canadian librarian who had started her blog after hearing a speaker on the subject of library blogs at the Ontario Library Association's Annual Super Conference, wanted to use her blog to support her continuous professional development and 'to stay informed about changes and developments in our field'. However, she found that this was not all she wanted to write about and that her life outside the library also appeared in her blog, making it more personal than her original intentions.

> I am a librarian, and I'm proud of my profession and what I do. I love my library dearly, all its little quirks and everything. I want to share with this audience in general what it is that I do, and try to convey what it is about this job that I love. However, while it is important to share what it's like behind the scenes in a smallish, public library, it's also important to remember that I have a life and other interests outside of my job and the library. So, while I will post job-related entries and the occasional "check this out!" I will also be posting trivial and off-topic stuff, too. (*Mary K Librarian*, 31 January 2004)

Ojala (2005) argues that there are two important aspects of blogging that make it particularly useful for knowledge sharing – their community and their archives. She points out that a major problem for knowledge managers in an organisation can be getting people to share their knowledge, but that blogging can help with this, making blogs an inexpensive way in which an organisation can encourage employees to share knowledge. Williams and Jacobs (2004) agree that informal systems like blogs can be easier to implement and maintain than formal knowledge management systems. However, again, both Ojala and Pedley emphasise the need for such blogging to be a grass-roots effort rather than being imposed by management. An internal knowledge blog needs to be viewed as non-threatening by its users – a peer-to-peer tool encouraging active and informal involvement in the process of knowledge sharing.

At least one of the survey respondents made the connection between information management and blogging. Perhaps not surprisingly he was a librarian who explained:

> I work as a library cataloguer, so organisation of information is relevant to blogging, e.g. I assign subject headings (mainly LCSH) which is similar to tagging. Also, and more generally, I have to write reports, e-mails and such like that are not dissimilar to writing in blog posts.

He reported that his blog attracted readers who were also library cataloguers or librarians with similar professional interests, supporting Pedley's contention that information professionals can gather information from the blogs of others in the same field.

However, the benefits of blogging as a way of storing and handling information were also acknowledged by survey respondents who were not professional information managers. Indeed, improvements in information handling can be an unforeseen benefit of blogging that impacts positively on a blogger's intention to continue blogging (Miura and Yamashita, 2007) while information handling has been identified as an important motivator for both blogging and constructing personal home pages (Chun-Yao et al., 2007; Papacharissi, 2002).

Just under half of all respondents (18 in 2006 and 49 in 2007) saw blogging as useful for sharing specialist knowledge with others, although a much smaller minority (two in 2007) specifically mentioned its use as an information or reference tool, suggesting that the information-management capabilities of blogging are at present mainly perceived by information professionals rather than members of the general public. The current dominance of the journal blog in the public blogosphere may mean that the importance of information gratifications in blogging has declined in comparison to motivations related to communication and interpersonal relationships. However, about a quarter of all respondents saw blogging as useful for their work or studies (12 in 2006 and 29 in 2007), which may imply an information-storage use of blogging.

Overall, however, the survey respondents had little to say about blogging as an information or knowledge management tool, suggesting that such motivations were not of primary importance in comparison to those related to communication and personal writing and that, while blogging has been celebrated as a useful and inexpensive tool for professional knowledge managers, such uses are of less conscious importance to the non-professional blogger.

Doing it for different reasons I: women's motivations for blogging

North American studies suggest that more than half of all blog authors are women, that they persevere longer and write more (Henning, 2003) and that at least 50 per cent of journal bloggers in particular are female (Herring et al., 2004). From the outset, journal blogs have been particularly associated with women. Women write more diary-like blogs while male bloggers write more of the opinion-focused ones (Herring and Paolillo, 2006).

One of the reasons for the number of women blogging is the fact that there are simply more women online. In fact, according to a Nielsen/Net Ratings report published in the UK in May 2007, young women aged between 18 and 34 are now the most dominant online group in the UK, marking a major shift from traditional male Internet dominance. It is suggested that British women in this age category spend, on average, around 60 hours a month online (Nielsen/Net Ratings, 2007). And women are using the Internet for different reasons to men. For example, they use e-mail more than men for communicating with family and friends and to strengthen family ties. It is suggested that women have always acted as the communication hubs between their household, family and friends and that now they have simply started to use the communication tools offered by the Internet for such purposes (Boneva and Kraut, 2002).

Women, and in particular mothers, are also more likely to search the internet for health information and educational purposes while men are more likely to search for news and entertainment. Allan and Rainie (2002) found that 70 per cent of US parents used the Internet compared to 53 per cent of non-parents and that parents were more likely to access health, lifestyle-enhancing and religious information. With society becoming increasingly mobile, parents are not able to rely on older sources of such information such as kinship structures, which may be geographically distant, and so there is an increasing reliance on advice garnered from parenting or health websites and discussion groups. While such sites tend to describe themselves as offering support and advice for parents, the vast majority of their users are mothers and not fathers. A survey about the use of the UK parenting website 'Mumsnet' garnered 391 responses, but only one was from a father (Pedersen and Smithson, 2009). As Sarkadi and Bremberg (2005) point out, even in Sweden, with relatively high gender equality and explicit social policies promoting involved fathering aimed at increasing fathers' involvement in childrearing, the lack of fathers as members of these parenting websites and respondents in related research is pointed.

The use of parenting-related online communities can impact positively on mothers' psychological well-being, supplementing rather than displacing real-life support (Miyata, 2002). Such sites provide virtual social support and alternative information sources for mothers, although they have also been criticised for reinforcing traditional stereotypes of mothering and unequal gender roles (Madge and O'Conner, 2006). Some sites also offer a virtual space in which working mothers can perform their maternal role identities whilst separated from their children (Hau-nung Chan, 2008).

Online parenting communities offer a place where mothers can not only find advice and support but also offer it to other mothers. Another place where such exchanges of knowledge take place is, of course, what have become known as 'mommy blogs'. In Technorati's report on the state of the blogosphere 2008 it was stated that of the 133 million existing blogs in the blogosphere, 36 per cent of female bloggers and 16 per cent of male were focused on family updates and that the most popular mommy blogs can attract more than 50,000 hits per day and collect hundreds of comments per entry (Sifry, 2008, quoted in Lopez, 2009). Like the real mothers using the discussion sites, mommy blogs offer their readers a 'warts and all' picture of motherhood somewhat in opposition to the traditional images of domestic bliss found elsewhere in the mainstream media (Lopez, 2009). Most mommy bloggers write in a humorous and down-to-earth way about the trials and tribulations of motherhood, whether they are stay-at-home moms (SAHM), working-out-of-the-home moms (WOHM), adoptive mothers or step-mothers.

It's nice to have discussions and build friendship when being a stay-at-home mum is quite lonely. (*Female respondent*, 2007)

As we have already seen, for a few A-list mommy bloggers such as Armstrong (*Dooce*) their writing can be extremely remunerative, with advertising sales around the blog and potential publishing deals to be factored in. As well as the collections mentioned in Chapter 6, books currently available from mommy bloggers include *Sleep Is for the Weak: The Best of the Mommybloggers* (Chicago Review Press, 2008); *The White Trash Mom Handbook* (St Martin's Griffin, 2008) and Elizabeth Soutter Schwarzer's *Motherhood is Not for Wimps* (Authorhouse, 2006) based on her blog of the same name. However, Lopez suggests that mommy bloggers can feel marginalised both by other women bloggers and by the blogosphere as a whole because of their choice of subject matter and, as already mentioned, have been particularly attacked for their collaboration with advertisers.

Male dominance

The substantial number of women bloggers and the success of the mommy bloggers have not, however, led to female dominance in the blogosphere – rather the opposite in fact. Research into the North American blogosphere has suggested that male bloggers tend to receive more links to their blogs from other bloggers (for references to the extensive online debate, see Pollard, 2003; Ratliff, 2004a, 2004b; Garfunkel, 2005). Having more links places a blog higher in the popularity ranks, and the effect is amplified by the use, by blog-monitoring sites such as Technorati, of page-ranking algorithms that give greater weight to links from blogs that are themselves highly ranked. Ratliff (2006) has also produced evidence that men's postings receive more comments than women's. It has also been claimed that a greater amount of attention is given in the media to male bloggers (Herring et al., 2004a; Pedersen and Macafee, 2006). For example, in the UK the apparent lack of women bloggers on political issues prompted Taylor (2004) to ask: 'Is Blog a Masculine Noun?' while Michael A Banks' book *Blogging Heroes: Interviews with 30 of the World's Top Bloggers* (John Wiley & Sons, 2007) includes interviews with 30 bloggers whom he considers to be influential, ground-breaking and successful, of whom 23 are male bloggers and only seven women.

There is, however, one area of media debate where female bloggers dominate: all discussion about sex blogging. Blogging about sex is dominated by women, possibly because the Internet offers a safe space within which women can express truths about their own sexuality (Attwood,

2009). However, sex blogging has low status in the blogosphere, viewed as a cheap trick with which to get more hits and links (Ray, 2007, quoted Attwood, 2009). In September 2006, the monthly issue of the UK *Observer Woman* magazine (a supplement to the *Observer* Sunday newspaper) ran an article on 'Confessional bloggers – the women whose sexploits reached thousands of readers' (Behr, 2006). This article identified five female bloggers, two of whom were British, including Belle de Jour. The article focused solely on sex-confessional blogging by women and made no mention of male bloggers at all. This prurient interest in women who blog about sex is, happily, not the only attention paid to women bloggers by the British media: the *Guardian*'s 'Women' page has run articles about feminist bloggers. Nevertheless, media coverage of blogging has focussed disproportionately on men, and female bloggers are usually presented as a minority, unless, of course, the subject under discussion is sexual confession, in which case 100 per cent of the bloggers discussed are women.

So on one hand we have evidence that at least half, if not more, of all bloggers – particularly journal bloggers – are women, but on the other hand researchers and the mainstream media are suggesting that the blogosphere is dominated by male bloggers. Why is this? One of the reasons suggested for such an imbalance is that blogs about technology and politics, which are popular subjects throughout the Internet, are more likely to be authored by men. It is also suggested that men are more likely to blog about external events, rather than personal ones, and are therefore more likely to be found by prospective readers when using a search engine. Such discussions have led to the establishment of the BlogHer movement in the United States with the mission to create opportunities for women bloggers to pursue exposure, education and community. However, it should be noted that Lopez suggests that it was at the inaugural BlogHer Conference in San Jose, California, in 2005 that mommy bloggers felt themselves to be particularly under attack for their style of blogging, leading one leading mommy blogger, Alice Bradley, who writes *Finslippy*, to declare: 'Mommy blogging *is* a radical act' (Lopez, 2009: 730).

What does seem certain is that the majority of bloggers – male and female – do not take the opportunities offered by the anonymity of the Internet to blur or switch gender. While the online world does offer individuals the opportunity to pretend to be the other sex in order to learn about their real self (Turkle, 1995), there is little evidence that such deception occurs frequently in the blogosphere. For example, Huffaker and Calvert's (2005) study of teenage bloggers found that they used their blogs as extensions of their real-life world rather than as places to pretend, although male teen bloggers might use their blog to safely discuss a homosexual identity. Similarly, van Doorn et al. (2007) found that their sample of Dutch and Flemish bloggers accurately presented their gender identity through narratives of their everyday lives. This lack of gender experimentation is presumably linked to the amount of personal information the average blogger offers on his or her blog and the key motivation of keeping in touch with offline family and friends. As described below, as part of my research project I investigated all links on each respondent's blogroll and noted sex and geographical location of all linked bloggers. There were very few occasions on which I was not able to ascertain sex, either through the 'About Me' section of the blog or through information in the posts themselves. Thus, most women bloggers make themselves identifiable as women in the blogosphere and therefore any differences in popularity or impact that can be discerned between women and men bloggers must be linked to their sex, to the subjects they blog about or to some particularly gendered way in which they blog.

Women's motivations for blogging

If female bloggers are different to male bloggers, at least with regard to their chances of popularity or success, are they also different in their motivations for blogging? Are there any specifically female motivations? Why are women attracted to blogging?

For the most part, there were no significant differences between the male and female respondents to the surveys. As described in previous chapters there was little difference between men and women in their choice of definitions of blogging: journalism, publishing, diary-keeping and creative writing. Men and women were also agreed that the role of blogging in their own lives was primarily as a leisure activity. For both sexes, things that they might be doing instead of blogging included looking for or doing paid work, watching TV, or reading, although women were marginally more likely to mention hobbies or creative writing as other activities. Men and women found the same range of satisfactions in blogging, particularly exercising their talents and clarifying their thinking, although men were more likely to see their blogging as participation in a democratic movement and we saw in Chapter 3 that men were slightly more likely to describe their blogging in terms of citizen journalism. The majority of both sexes also agreed that they used blogging to vent their emotions or frustrations.

It has been suggested that men are more avid consumers than women of online information, while women are more enthusiastic online communicators (Fallows, 2005). If we see women as the communication hubs in a household, then Web 2.0 offers them Internet-based tools, such as social networking sites, e-mail and blogs, that help to fulfil social and interpersonal goals (Stefanone and Jang, 2007). Many of the differences in findings between male and female bloggers did reflect the greater importance for women of the social aspects of blogging. As seen in Tables 4.1 and 4.2, women were slightly more likely than men to encourage real-life friends to blog and to look at the blogs of their real-life friends.

> A close friend used to contribute articles to a blog. Then she started her own blog. I felt the need to keep up and so began blogging. She was very supportive and often tells me how much she likes my blog. (*Female respondent*, 2007)

Women were also more likely to belong to a blog-ring (a combined total of 45 women admitted belonging to at least one blog-ring in comparison to 28 men). Blog-rings connect a circle of blogs with a common theme or purpose. A link to the blog-ring is displayed on a blog and clicking on that link takes the reader to the blog-ring's page, where the other members of the blog-ring are listed. Alternatively, clicking on the link takes the reader directly to the next blog in the ring. For women, the most popular blog-rings were those that linked them to other bloggers of the same sex such as 'Blogs by Women' or 'Crazy/Hip Blog Mamas'. As one female respondent commented about blog-rings:

> You can feel like you are not the only person obsessed with [name of topic], but are instead part of a worldwide community that shares that interest.

Male bloggers were more likely to belong to a blog-ring that promoted an interest or hobby, such as blog-rings for birdwatchers, Methodists or transvestites, which reflects the male bloggers' preference for issue-based blogging, while female bloggers were more likely to belong to blog-rings that celebrated their femininity, which again reflects the female proclivity for more journal blogging with a focus on themselves.

Given the fact that diary-writing has always been seen as a feminine genre, it is not surprising that women respondents were slightly more likely to state that their blog had replaced a paper diary (26 women and 14 men). However, as we have already discussed, the essential difference between the traditional diary and a blog is dialogue with one's readers and I would suggest that it is the validation offered by such feedback that is one of the main motivators for women who write journal blogs. Readers' comments on women's journal blogs are almost always supportive: either contrasting the blogger's experience to their own, offering advice or simply using the oft-repeated phrase 'you go, girl!' It is noticeable that commentators are usually similarly situated and therefore feel an instant connection to the blogger's experience. Perhaps this is not an unexpected finding. Working mothers comment on the blogs of other working mothers, ditto stay-at-home moms or home educators. Supportive comments on sites dedicated to miscarriages or attempts to conceive come from other women in the same situation. On rare occasions, a negative comment might be made. The useful thing about a blog is that the blogger is the editor and can immediately remove such a comment – thus making the 'public' sphere more 'private' again. However, in the time that this comment existed, the blogger is usually inundated by many more supportive comments than usual.

In early September I did a brief post on my unhappiness at the situation in Lebanon and government inertia. I did 'apologise' in advance for putting this on the blog, as I normally post about 'nice things'. But other women bloggers had felt that they had to speak out – even if just once – in a similar vein, and I was supporting them and putting my own small voice 'out there' saying that in my opinion, it was wrong and barbaric. I got 99 per cent support for this in my comments, apart from one regular reader, who chose to remain 'anonymous' although it was obvious from what they wrote that they knew me. They called me by my real name, Gretel, (which is not on my blog) and they stated that they thought that such things did not belong on an 'art blog' and that they came to my blog to 'get away from that kind of thing'. They also apologised for saying it! I gave a brief reply, in a friendly tone, and left it at that – as I suspected would happen, many blogger friends and people I'd never had visit before, leapt to my defence and said how outrageous it was that someone should try to tell me what to put on my blog, and to remain anonymous as well. I found it very unsettling, as it showed me how much 'ownership' people think they have over popular blogs and reinforced my desire to keep my whereabouts vague. I have noticed that on very very popular blogs, such as 'Petite Anglaise' or 'Waiterant' that regular commenters are all too happy to leap to the defence of the blogger, and there is no need for the blogger to get involved in a heated argument, as others will do it for them – which is why I left it to others to say what I really felt, and thankfully, they did! (*Female respondent*, 2007)

Margaret Beetham (2006) has compared the blogging of modern-day women to the letters written to women's magazines in the second half of the nineteenth century, such as *Woman at Home* and *Englishwoman's Review*. While Beetham makes some excellent points about the similarities between the two media opening the possibility to women of making their opinions known to a wider audience, I would suggest that a better comparison is with women who were consciously stepping outside the woman's domestic sphere to involve themselves in debate in the much more public sphere of daily newspapers. Both blogs and newspaper correspondence are ways in which a woman could or can make her opinions known to people (both men and women) outside her particular domestic circle. While women bloggers are predominantly 'journal' bloggers, writing about personal events rather than commenting on external ones, many female correspondents to the early twentieth century newspapers also chose to write about matters pertaining to their home, their families or the domestic economy, justifying their entrance into publication by reference to their role as mothers or wives. However, as we have seen in the above-mentioned quote, even the most domestic journal bloggers can sometimes choose to enter into debate about issues such as politics and religion using the safe space of their blog, just as early women political activists such as the suffragettes used letters to the newspapers as a way of making their voices heard and their arguments clear even in conservative publications.

Table 8.1	The usefulness of blogging by sex (combined totals from surveys 2006 and 2007)		
	Women	Men	All
Brings custom for your business	18	11	29
Widens the audience for your intellectual work	26	34	60
Widens the audience for your creative work	47	34	81
Other	30	19	49
None	5	9	14

As far as the *usefulness* of blogging was concerned, women were slightly more likely to emphasise creative work and men to focus on their intellectual work.

It is interesting to note that more women than men saw blogging as bringing custom for their business. This may be related to the fact that more women respondents worked part time and in the home. Giving combined totals for both years of the survey, 27 female respondents described themselves as working part-time in comparison to 10 male respondents while 30 female respondents described their home as their place of employment in comparison to 19 male respondents. It seems that women based in the home, perhaps because of caring or other responsibilities, might use their blogs to support the establishment of freelance or part-time work.

> It has created an opportunity for me to supplement my income from home doing something I enjoy. (*Female respondent*, 2006)

> I also find that having a large amount of people visiting my blog has been a tremendous motivator for doing new artwork and publicising my professional projects. At the moment I am using my blog to advertise my forthcoming Christmas cards, and am generating sales through it. (*Female respondent*, 2007)

Blogroll differences

One part of the 2007 project investigated in greater detail the respondents' blogrolls. This part of the project was based on a short analysis of blogrolls undertaken for the 2006 respondents, which had suggested that women bloggers were more likely to recommend other women's blogs than male bloggers, which is presumably linked to the subject matter of male and female blogs (see Pedersen and Macafee, 2006). In 2007 I wished to examine this proposition in more detail. The blogroll is a collection or list of favourite links to other blogs and is a common feature on blogs. They are sometimes referred to as 'link lists' or bookmarks. All blogroll links were followed and analysed in terms of who was writing the linked blog (man, woman or a group of bloggers) and geographical location. As will be seen, the findings agreed with the original proposition that male bloggers are more likely to recommend only other male bloggers to their readers while female bloggers are more likely to link to both male and female bloggers.

The average blogroll is not a long list of links. Fifty-eight (71 per cent) of the blogrolls analysed had ten or fewer links. Interestingly, the US male respondents were more likely to have longer blogrolls, only ten (33 per cent) having ten or fewer links. American male bloggers were also responsible for the two longest blogrolls in the survey, with 206 and 425 links. However, at least a quarter of the longest blogroll was made up of links that did not work, suggesting that the blogger continued to add links to his blogroll without checking or pruning previous recommendations. Indeed, the whole idea that the blogroll represents the recommended reading or favourite reads of a blogger becomes a nonsense when a blogroll is this long. In addition, many of these excessively long blogrolls appear to have taken a large amount of their content from an extant list, for example the 'Methodist blogroll', which two respondents used, and therefore their blogrolls do not reflect personal selection but rather an interest in or commitment to a particular group of bloggers. The Methodist blogroll, for example, invites readers to add their own blog to the list, thus encouraging a lengthy blogroll. This problem was acknowledged by one US male blogger who is a minister. His blogroll was divided into two sections. The first, and shorter, section was called 'Daily reads' and seemed to be his personal recommendations, while the second was the 'Blogroll of Reformed Bloggers' and again was a self-nomination blogroll linked to his particular religious beliefs. There seemed to be a connection between long blogrolls and religious interests. A fourth blogger with a long blogroll was an evangelical Christian from the United States who worked as a member of an online evangelical ministry. Most of the blogs in his blogroll were religious in nature.

Several female respondents on both sides of the pond were members of another self-nomination blogroll, 'Women who blog', which was made up of 110 links, all of them to female blogs, but again with a high number of failed links or abandoned blogs – just under a third (30 failed links). Again, just as with the blog-rings, it was noticeable that women bloggers chose to emphasise their gender when joining self-nomination blogrolls while the male bloggers joined blogrolls related to their interests, whether that was religion or bird-watching. This again can be related to the journal/filter division, with many women choosing to write journal blogs with an internal focus on their own lives and families rather than externally focused filter blogs. The promotion of women's blogging that we see in organisations such as BlogHer may also have played a part in ensuring that female bloggers are more conscious of their gender in the wider blogosphere.

Not all long blogrolls were the result of the use of self-nomination blogrolls, however. Other bloggers took a more personal approach to their blogroll. For example, a UK male respondent who discussed his mental health problems on his blog had a particularly long blogroll with many links relating to mental health. However, his blogroll was in no sense a one-issue set of links, and he also had many links relating to his other interests in politics and cultural issues. A US female blogger who wrote columns for local newspapers in her home state offered a long list of bloggers based in that state. One respondent who took a very active interest in tending his blogroll was a US male blogger with an interest in birdwatching. He aims to produce the definitive list of birding blogs and has made some thoughtful posts about birding blogs worldwide, including one state-by-state analysis of all the American birding blogs to which he links. However, even his blogroll of 206 links had a 15 per cent failure rate, demonstrating how difficult it is for a blogger to stay on top of all the links in a long blogroll. The blogs with longer blogrolls tended to be associated with a particular interest or hobby; in other words, were 'filter' blogs. Longer blogrolls were much less likely to appear on the more diary-like journal blogs.

All links on the blogroll were followed and the sex of the linked blogger ascertained. This was usually discovered by reading the blogger's profile or reading through the blog for sex-specific information such as 'my pregnancy' or 'night out with the lads'. It was usually easy to discover the sex of a blogger, but blogs were not counted in this analysis if it was not possible to accurately decide the sex of the writer or if the linked blog was a group blog written by more than one person. There is in fact a website which professes to be able to discern the sex of a blogger with 80 per cent accuracy called 'Gender Genie' (*http://bookblog.net/gender/genie.php*). Gender Genie uses a simplified version of an algorithm developed by Koppel and Argamon to predict the gender of an author. You put a piece of text in (they recommend that it is over 500 words for the most accurate results), choose whether it is fiction, non-fiction or a blog entry, and then ask the program to analyse the words and indicate the gender it thinks the writer is. Herring and Paolillo discuss the Gender Genie approach in an article on gender and genre variation in blogs (2006). Out of interest, I tried Gender Genie out on my UK respondents. For the male bloggers, it identified 70 per cent correctly, but for the female bloggers only 46 per cent. While Gender Genie does not analyse the subjects of posts, but rather the language, it was amusing to discover that it could decide that a woman blogging about going for her first pregnancy scan

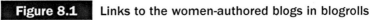
Figure 8.1   Links to the women-authored blogs in blogrolls

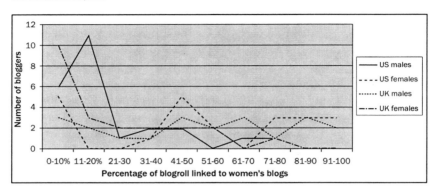

was male! (Columnist Alexander Chancellor of *The Guardian* newspaper utilised the Gender Genie to analyse samples of his colleagues' work in 2003 and also found that it correctly identified all his male colleagues but could only correctly identify one of his female colleagues, which suggests that this may be an on-going issue for the developers (Chancellor, 2003).)

Figure 8.1 shows the percentage of bloggers' blogrolls linked to women's blogs, broken down by nationality and gender. Perhaps not surprisingly, women bloggers were more likely to link to other female bloggers. However, the extent to which male bloggers, plus some women, ignored female blogs was surprising.

Of the 46 male bloggers who had blogrolls, twelve had no links at all to blogs written by women, in other words their blogroll was 100 per cent male-authored blogs. In addition, of the 43 female bloggers who had blogrolls, eight had no links to female bloggers. Four of the female bloggers had 100 per cent of their links to women-authored blogs. In all, thirty male bloggers had less than 20 per cent of their links to female-authored bloggers while only five male bloggers and 22 female blogs had over 50 per cent of their links to female bloggers. This indicates that male bloggers are more likely to be linked to via the blogroll and confirms earlier research by myself and Macafee (2006) and Henning (2003), who stated that women's blogs make up only 15 per cent of all blogrolls. While female bloggers tend to link to both male and female bloggers, male bloggers are more likely to link only to male bloggers.

Previous work focusing on the North American blogosphere has suggested that male bloggers dominate this part of the blogosphere for a number of reasons. These include the likelihood that they blog about external rather than personal events; their enthusiasm for promoting their blog; and the linkage between male blogs. The present study has confirmed that male bloggers are more likely to recommend other male bloggers to their readers and more likely to be writing about external rather than personal events: i.e. filter rather than journal bloggers. Female bloggers, who are more likely to write journal blogs, are less likely to be linked to by other blogs, and this puts them at a disadvantage in terms of popularity in the blogosphere. Does this matter? If the average woman blogger is motivated to blog for communication and support purposes rather than to impress her opinions or expertise in public affairs on others, then does it matter that she has only a limited readership and few links from other blogs? If she is blogging about family and friends and personal domestic issues then it is perhaps not surprising that her readership is smaller than that of another blogger who writes about more external, public affairs. There is one aspect of the matter that might concern this woman blogger and perhaps lead her to change her blogging style – the money motive. As we have seen, there is a growing financial motivation in the blogosphere and many of the female survey respondents admitted that they hoped to use their blogs to earn additional income for their household. They usually hoped to raise this money through hosting advertising on their blogs – and advertisers tend to be attracted to blogs with a proven readership.

It therefore seems that while female bloggers share a lot of the same motivations for blogging as male bloggers, there are certain motivations that may be particularly linked to women. Given that women are more likely to write journal blogs it is not surprising to find the diary motivation important for women bloggers. In the same way, women are using blogs to continue their role as the household communicator with family and friends. However, this motivation can sometimes be at odds with concerns about revealing too much online. As was discussed in the chapter on privacy, women are more likely than men to have concerns about privacy on the Internet as a whole and also within their blogs, and this leads to them being careful with the personal information they release in their posts. They are particularly concerned about being identified by strangers because of details on their blog.

Women are appreciative of the way in which blogging offers them a way to showcase their creativity online – especially when such show-casing can coincide with a way in which to make some extra income. Women who do not leave the home to work, perhaps because they are acting as carers for children or other family members, might also use their blog to market their freelance skills or in some other way raise additional income for the family.

Finally, women are appreciative of the support they gain from their online communication with others in the same type of situation as them. With the advent of Web 2.0 women are using online communication tools such as blogs, e-mail and social networking sites to communicate with other women in similar situations, to offer and accept support and advice and to gain validation of their own opinions from outside the domestic circle.

Doing it for different reasons II: Americans and Brits

At first restricted mainly to North America, blogging is now a worldwide phenomenon: 33 per cent of the posts tracked by Technorati in October 2006 were in Japanese, whereas only 39 per cent were in English (Sifry, 2006b). While our 2006 survey focused on the differences between British male and female bloggers, the second survey in 2007 included both British and American respondents – 60 from each country. Although the study found much that was similar in blogging on both sides of the pond, certain differences between British and American bloggers were established, in particular relating to their motivations for blogging, how the bloggers perceived blogging and satisfactions gained from blogging. These differences were particularly noticeable when gender was also factored in, leading to the conclusion that the main differences to be ascertained were actually not between men and women or between the American and the British bloggers but between the Amercian male bloggers and the rest of the survey participants.

Demographic differences

The age of the respondents ranged from 18 to 73 years, with the British respondents being slightly younger than the American. Forty per cent of the British respondents were under 30, in comparison with 26 per cent of the American respondents, and 4 per cent of the British respondents were over 56, with the American figure being 18 per cent. Thus, for this random sample, the American bloggers were, on average, older than the British bloggers. However, there was no perceptible difference in the amount of time each group had been blogging. The differences between the two countries were, however, found in terms of educational attainment, with the American respondents having, on average, a higher educational attainment. Forty-seven per cent of the American respondents were educated to bachelor degree level, compared with 32 per cent of the British respondents, and 35 per cent of the American respondents held a postgraduate degree, in comparison with 18 per cent of the British respondents. Twenty-eight per cent of the British respondents reported that their highest level of educational attainment was as a school leaver compared with only 10 per cent of the American respondents. To a certain extent, this must be linked to the fact that the British respondents were younger than the American respondents, although it should be noted that 11 British respondents were currently undertaking education compared with 13 American respondents.

Previous studies into the blogosphere have characterised bloggers as usually educated to graduate level or beyond. Some of these studies even focused on university bloggers through their selection of survey participants, which may, of course, have impacted on the findings. For example, Schiano (2004) interviewed bloggers in and around Stanford University, Guadagno et al. (2008) studied students from a large south-eastern university in the United States and Menchen-Trevino interviewed 14 college student bloggers. Their findings have been supported by larger-scale surveys such as Technorati's recent (2009) report on the *State of the Blogosphere* – based on a survey of 2,828 bloggers, half of whom were from the United States – which found that 75 per cent of the respondents had college degrees and 40 per cent had graduate degrees. Therefore, it may be suggested that the second wave of blogging outside the United States is attracting a different type of person to the blogosphere. Is blogging in the United Kingdom more associated with youth culture?

Perceptions of blogging

The first difference to be discerned was in the *perception* of blogging by the respondents: whether it was seen as a form of creative writing or was more related to information technology (IT). The respondents were asked to indicate whether any of the following skills used in their current employment were necessary for their blogging: IT skills, journalism or creative writing. They were allowed to select as many of these three skills as they wanted, or to suggest others.

As can be seen in Figure 9.1, the British respondents were far more likely than the American respondents to see the IT skills used in their

Figure 9.1 Skills necessary for current job and relevant to blogging (by country)

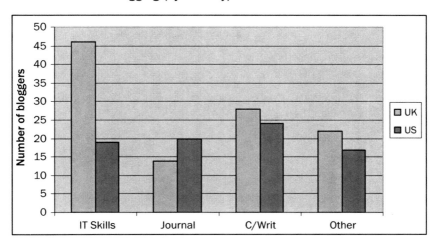

current employment as relevant to their blogging, with 46 out of a possible 54 respondents (85 per cent) clicking the IT skills button, compared with 26 out of a possible 51 (50 per cent) of American respondents seeing the IT skills used in their current employment as relevant to their blogging or even using such skills in their current jobs. The American respondents were more likely to see their creative writing skills as useful for their blogging. In particular, the American male respondents felt that they brought creative writing skills from their employment to blogging, as demonstrated in Figure 9.2, in which the respondents are categorised by both country and sex.

Further evidence of this IT/creative divide can be found in the 'other skills' category that respondents could select in answer to this question. Six British respondents gave further details of particular IT skills they used in blogging and in their job, such as webpage designing or the use of specific software programs, in comparison with only two American respondents, both women. Four American respondents mentioned that they used marketing and promotion skills from their work in their blogging, but no British respondent mentioned such skills. When asked about other forms of computer-mediated communication they used, the British respondents were far more likely to admit their experiences with tools such as listservs, chatrooms or bulletin boards than the American respondents, who were even less experienced with e-mail than the British bloggers (see Figure 9.3).

These results suggest that the American respondents, and the American male respondents in particular, saw blogging as a much more creative

Figure 9.2 Skills necessary for current job and relevant to blogging (by country and sex)

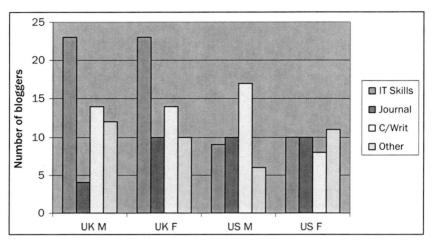

Figure 9.3 Other forms of computer-mediated communication used by respondents, by country, 2007

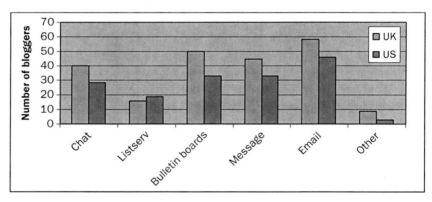

process than the British, who saw it as more of an IT-based phenomenon. This conclusion was further strengthened when the respondents were asked what they would be doing if they weren't blogging (see Figure 9.4).

The British respondents were more likely to mention surfing the Internet, watching television or working as alternatives to blogging, whereas the American respondents were more likely to mention reading, creative writing and, in particular, writing in their journal, something no British respondent

Figure 9.4 What would you do with your time if you didn't blog?

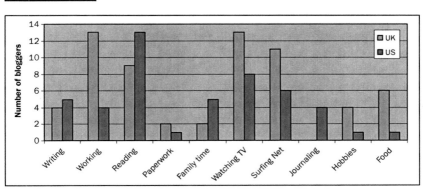

mentioned. In addition, more American than British respondents found that blogging widened the audience for both their creative work (36 American, 26 British) and their intellectual work (25 American, 14 British).

Comments from the American respondents also emphasised the importance of blogging as a form of creative writing. As one female respondent explained:

> It satisfies my need to express myself through writing. ... I feel compelled to write and blogging is a wonderful way to do that. I have written two books in the past and that is very hard work; blogging is more enjoyable and less demanding. I like the essay genre and blogging is perfect for short little essays about anything under the sun.

A young male respondent from the United States said: 'If you write, you will find it easy to blog. Mostly, because that's all blogging is. Writing.' In comparison, a British blogger, who actually focused her blog on literary criticism, made an explicit link between her blog and IT:

> It keeps me current and relevant in this technological world. I love it. At 54 years of age, I know more about computers and such than many others much younger than me.

It should be noted, however, that although the American male respondents were happy to see their blogging as a form of creative writing, they were less likely to see blogging as a form of diary-keeping. In response to the question asking whether blogging was a form of diary-keeping, journalism, publishing or other, only 12 American men selected diary-keeping in comparison with 23 American women, 21 British men and 21 British women.

The connection that the British respondents made between blogging and IT is supported by the findings of a study by Efimova (2003) on what she calls the 'stickiness factor' of blogging, by which she means the likelihood of a blogger continuing to blog after the initial start-up period. She argues that blogging fits well with jobs that require studying or using technology in general or using blogs, in particular, for learning, collaboration or knowledge sharing. It is interesting that the British respondents agree with Efimova and the connection she makes between IT and blogging. The British bloggers' focus on IT is also interesting in the light of the fact that the majority of the respondents from both countries can be said to be in the second wave of blogging, which occurred after the introduction of the easy-to-use/build-your-own-blog software such as Blogger in 1999, and therefore they have little need for advanced computing skills for their blogging. Analysing how long all the respondents had been blogging shows that 62 – over half – had been blogging for less than two years and that these beginners were evenly spread throughout the two countries. Only one-third of the respondents, again spread evenly between the two countries, had been blogging for over three years. Therefore, the vast majority of the respondents would never have needed advanced programming skills in order to blog.

Satisfactions from blogging

The respondents were asked to select any number of choices from a list of statements about the satisfaction they gained from blogging, and Figure 9.5 shows their responses (divided into the two nationalities).

As can be seen, the most popular statements were blogging as a way of 'exercising talents' and blogging as a way of 'clarifying thinking'. Ignoring the two British respondents who claimed to find no satisfaction at all in blogging (then why do it?), the least popular statements were 'redressing the biases of the media' (32 respondents) and blogging as a 'democratic movement' (28 respondents). It is noticeable that, overall, the American respondents were more willing to admit finding a variety of satisfactions in their blogging, with the American selecting 502 choices compared with the British (420 choices). As can be seen from Figure 9.5, the British respondents equalled the American respondents only in their enthusiasm for blogging as

Figure 9.5 Satisfactions gained from blogging (by country)

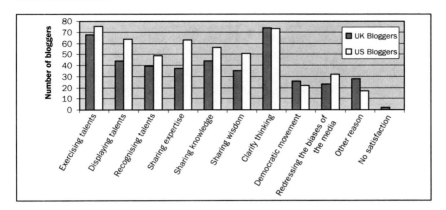

Figure 9.6 Satisfactions gained from blogging (by country and sex)

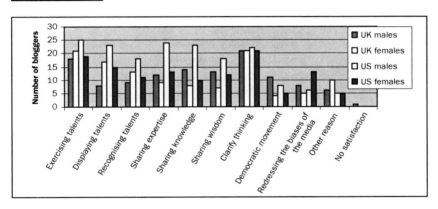

a way of 'clarifying thinking' and were more enthusiastic than the Americans only in finding satisfaction with blogging as a 'democratic movement'. The satisfactions that the American respondents were particularly enthusiastic about included 'exercising talents', 'displaying talents' and 'sharing expertise'. With regard to gender and country, again the American male respondents stood out in comparison with the other respondents, as is shown in Figure 9.6, in which the respondents are categorised by sex and country.

The American male respondents selected more choices of satisfactions from blogging than any other group (172 in comparison with the next highest group, the American women, who made 124 choices) and also found far more satisfaction in 'sharing expertise' and 'sharing knowledge' than any other group.

What does this mean? Why might the American male bloggers be so satisfied with the blogging experience? Part of the methodology of this project was to rank the 120 respondents' blogs in terms of popularity using data gathered from the blog-monitoring sites Technorati and The Truth Laid Bear and information concerning the number of links made to a blog's front page from Surfwax. The Truth Laid Bear (*http:// truthlaidbear.com*) and Technorati (*http://www.technorati.com*) are websites that use links from other blogs as the measure of the relative worth of a blog. Surfwax is a metasearch engine whose Site Snaps function offers a quick abstract of any web page, including the number of links made to that page. Since popularity, as demonstrated by the number of links made to a blog, is used as the main criterion for success in the blogosphere, the surveyed blogs were ranked using the data collected and then the top and bottom 20 blogs in the listing were analysed to discern any common characteristics.

The top 20 blogs in terms of popularity were written by 12 American respondents (10 men and 2 women) and 8 British respondents (4 men and 4 women). The bottom 20 blogs were written by 8 American respondents (1 man and 7 women) and 12 British respondents (6 men and 6 women). If we accept that popularity equals success in the blogosphere, then what is suggested by this quick exercise is that the American male respondents were, on average, more successful in the blogosphere than the other three groups.

The Surfwax data were also used to rank the bloggers in terms of the number of links, number of images and number of words used in their blogs. In terms of the number of links, again the American men dominated, with six blogs in the top ten compared with two British men, one British woman and one American woman. These included a birding enthusiast, an evangelical Christian, an expert in global current affairs, an expert on German culture and an expert on American football. The two British men included another Christian, this time a minister, and a blogger with a long blogroll relating to mental illness. Both the female bloggers (one British and one American) were promoting their businesses through the Internet, one as a children's book illustrator and the other as a sex therapist. If a high number of links in the blog is used as an indicator of success in the blogosphere, then again we have more successful American male bloggers, but it is also obvious that bloggers who focused on one particular subject, which may or may not be related to their career or a source of income, were the most active in terms of links. Out of the ten most successful bloggers, five were writing about some aspect of their career. This agrees with the findings of Herring et al. (2004) that journal blogs, focused on the blogger's personal life, tend to have fewer links than filter blogs.

In terms of the number of images used on the blogs, the top ten bloggers included seven American men, two British women and one American woman. Four of these ten bloggers were also in the list of blogs with a high number of links (mentioned previously): the birding expert, the international affairs expert (who wrote for a variety of magazines and journals on the subject), the evangelical Christian and another blogger whose blog focused on funny and strange things to be found on the Internet. One British female blogger used her blog as part of her online shop that sold objects for the home and therefore illustrations and photos in the blog were very necessary. It appears that the American bloggers were happier, or more technically able, to use photos on their blogs than the British bloggers. In comparison, Herring's team found relatively low levels of image use in their study of the American bloggers, but this can probably be explained by the developments in access to and ease of use of digital cameras in the few years between the two studies (Herring et al., 2004: 9).

The ten blogs with the largest number of words in recent postings belonged to six American men, two British men, one American woman and one British woman. Again, most of these blogs were filter blogs with a theme or focus. Of the two female bloggers, one discussed right-wing politics, whereas the other reviewed crime novels. One of the two British men wrote about military affairs, having been a soldier, whereas the other was a policeman writing anonymously about policing in the United Kingdom. Of the six American men, two were religious bloggers, one wrote about international affairs, one was the expert on American football, one was a soldier writing about military affairs and one was a German expatriate blogging about international culture.

As can be ascertained from these descriptions, many of the bloggers who were in the top ten ranking for the largest number of words were also in the top ten ranking for the highest number of either images or links. The two bloggers who were in the top ten ranking in all three categories were the young American evangelical Christian and the American male who wrote about international politics, with an emphasis on technology. The bloggers in the top ten ranking for at least two out of the three categories were the birding enthusiast (American male), the German expatriate living in the United States and writing about cultural issues (American male), a group blog on American sports and betting (American male) and a minister writing from a Christian viewpoint (American male). Thus, all the dominant bloggers in the survey, according to the Surfwax data, were men based in the United States.

Is it any wonder then that the American male respondents were most likely to find a high number of satisfactions from their blogging or that such satisfactions were related to demonstrations of their knowledge, wisdom or expertise? As one American male respondent described:

> Blogging expands the sphere of my life and puts me in contact with people in every corner of the world. In a small way I am contributing to the larger pool of common knowledge and ideas in a world that is highly competitive in these matters. I have personally grown in my knowledge and understanding of world events, politics, religious faith through my blogging experience.

The finding that all the dominant bloggers in the 2007 study were American men corresponds to the general tenor of research findings about gender in blogging and the dominance of male bloggers in the American blogosphere, as already discussed in Chapter 8. It is therefore suggested by the findings of this survey that such a dominance of male bloggers in the United States, as identified by many commentators in the last few years, also translates into a dominance of the international, Anglophone blogosphere.

Blogroll differences

As explained in Chapter 8, the blogrolls of the respondents of the 2007 survey were analysed with respect to gender and geographical location of the blogs they linked to. In the survey, the respondents were asked what they had in common with the contacts on their blogroll. A variety of options was offered and the respondents were allowed to choose as many as they wished. Figure 9.7 shows the responses to this question.

As can be seen, the most popular choice here was 'interests' (92 respondents). Just under half, 59 respondents, also chose 'sense of humour'. The least popular choice was 'economic or domestic circumstances', with only eight respondents. 'Part of the world' was also an unpopular choice with only 19 respondents. The respondents did not perceive themselves as only linking to other bloggers who lived in the same part of the world as they did. With these results in mind, an analysis of the blogrolls of all respondents was undertaken in order to ascertain how willing the bloggers really were to link to blogs from outside their own country.

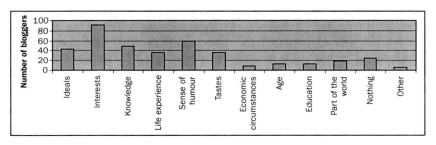

Figure 9.7 What do the contacts on your blogroll have in common with you?

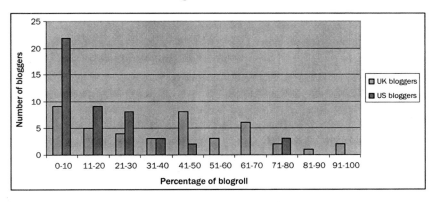

Figure 9.8 Percentage of bloggers' blogrolls containing links to overseas blogs

All links on the blogroll were followed and the geographical location of the linked blogger was ascertained, if possible. This was usually easily discovered by reading the blogger's profile or reading through blog entries. The results are shown in Figure 9.8.

Of the 47 American blogs that carried a blogroll, 31 (66 per cent) had less than 20 per cent of their blogroll links to blogs from outside the United States. In fact, 15 of these blogs had no links *at all* to blogs from outside the United States. The male blogger with the most links to blogs outside the United States was the German expatriate living in the United States who wrote a blog on international affairs and culture, primarily in German. He was the only respondent in the survey whose blog linked to non-English-language blogs. The female blogger with the most links to blogs located outside the United States wrote a blog focused on the work of Jane Austen and so linked to several British blogs on the subject.

Only three American bloggers had more than 50 per cent of links in their blogrolls to blogs outside the United States.

In comparison, of the British blogs, only 14 out of the 43 that featured blogrolls had less than 20 per cent of their blogroll linked to blogs from outside the United Kingdom. Of these, seven had no links to any blogs located outside the United Kingdom, whereas 14 bloggers had more than 50 per cent of their links to blogs outside the United Kingdom. Of course, it is not that surprising that the British bloggers link more to blogs outside the United Kingdom because there *are* more blogs outside the United Kingdom. Riley estimated in July 2005 that there were 2.5 million British bloggers compared with up to 30 million American bloggers, although there are difficulties in enumerating specifically British blogs because of what Riley calls 'the Anglosphere problem', i.e. the existence of a common body of service providers and readership across the English-speaking Internet (Riley, 2005), and while the figures have certainly changed since that time, the proportions are probably still quite similar.

However, the limited amount of linking that the average American blogger does to blogs from outside the United States should be noted. Is this a product of, or even part of the creation of a particular national identity on the part of these American bloggers? Do these bloggers, who have their own particular world view, seek out other blogs to read which are relevant to that view and, if so, why do the British not confine themselves to the British blogosphere in similar numbers? It is significant that, whenever an American blogger *did* link to blogs located outside the United States, these blogs were frequently written by either an expatriate or a member of the US forces serving there. For example, one American female blogger explained:

> I started out blogging as a way to keep friends up to date about my move to a foreign country. I had about three readers. I now have about 200 regular readers and am back in the US. My blog has gone from being the American in Sweden blog, to the substitute teacher blog to the wedding blog to the pregnancy blog and is now the baby blog. It has changed as my life has changed (I've been blogging for about five years).

Although bloggers might prefer to link to other bloggers in their own country, there was less evidence that they preferred to link to bloggers within their own state or town. Sixty-four per cent of all bloggers had less than 10 per cent of their blogroll devoted to links to other blogs in their local area. Only 8 per cent had more than 50 per cent of the links in their blogroll devoted to local blogs. However, all four of the bloggers whose links were 100 per cent local were from the USA and only two British bloggers had more than 50 per cent of their blogroll devoted to local links.

One of the ways in which nations set themselves apart from other nations is through the special nature of their internal communications. The media has always been a key element in the historical process of building national cultures and therefore it cannot be surprising that new media such as blogs can contribute to the self-perception of a nation, even if such a contribution is mainly to reflect back a self-image.

Interestingly, while British bloggers were more willing to link to blogs from outside the United Kingdom in their blogrolls, they were also more likely to be members of geographically defined blogrings. Blogrings connect a circle of blogs with a common theme or purpose. Twenty-five British respondents (11 men and 14 women) admitted to using blogrings, in comparison with 15 American respondents, only five of whom were male. The more popular blogrings were either those that linked bloggers of the same sex, such as 'Blogs by Women' or 'Crazy/Hip Blog Mamas', or those that linked bloggers in the same geographical location. Twenty-four bloggers linked to blogrings related to location, such as 'Blogging Brits', 'Scots Bloggers' or 'Expat Bloggers'. The relative popularity of blogrings among the British bloggers – and the high number of blogrings related to the United Kingdom or the regions of the country – is noteworthy in comparison with the lower interest from the American bloggers, in particular American male bloggers, and may point to a desire among the British bloggers to mark themselves out as different, or a need to group together, in the face of the much more numerous American bloggers.

Thus, investigating the geographical location of links in the blogrolls showed that the American bloggers were far more likely to link to other American bloggers, whereas the British bloggers were more willing to recommend overseas blogs to their readers, including a high number of American blogs. Part of the reason for this, of course, is that there are so many more American bloggers in the Anglophone blogosphere. However, it may also be evidence of a need to reflect back to the blogger a particular image of their national identity. British bloggers' comparative willingness to link to American bloggers may also indicate a wider knowledge of the United States and US politics and culture on their part in comparison with the American bloggers' knowledge of the equivalent overseas.

The findings of this section of the project therefore suggest that bloggers outside the United States may have different approaches to blogging and find different satisfactions in their blogging compared with the American bloggers. The American bloggers in this study were, on average, older than the British bloggers and differences between the two countries were also found in terms of educational attainment, suggesting that the picture of bloggers as, on average, educated to graduate level gained from earlier US-based studies needs to be questioned by more research into the blogosphere outside the United States.

In terms of the promotion of their blog, the British respondents were more likely to use blogrings. While the American respondents tended to dismiss blogrings as of less use than blog directories, the British bloggers were happy to use them, in particular those that identified the blogger as part of the United Kingdom or its regions. Given the very different sizes of the American and British blogosphere, this may well be in order for the British bloggers to identify each other and to maintain a sense of British identity against the overwhelming American group. The British bloggers were also more ready to make links to overseas blogs in their blogrolls, whereas the American bloggers, as a group, were less ready. More American bloggers also had blogrolls that contained only local links. Obviously, a great part of the explanation for this is the size of the American blogosphere compared with the rest of the world. It will be interesting to see if this US-centric approach changes in the future as the blogosphere continues to expand.

The American bloggers were more likely than the British bloggers to see blogging as a useful activity, attracting readers for their intellectual or creative work. Overall, the project suggests that further research needs to be undertaken into the blogosphere outside the United States. Because blogging started in the United States, the majority of research into blogging so far has focused on the United States and it is suggested that this focus has resulted in all bloggers being defined through the US experience. The findings of this project suggest that bloggers outside the United States may have different approaches to blogging and find different satisfactions.

Note

Sections of this chapter first appeared in Pedersen, S. (2008). Now read this: Male and female bloggers' recommendations for further reading. *Particip@tions: Journal of Audience and Reception Research*, 5(2) and Pedersen, S. (2007). Speaking the same language? Differences and similarities between US and UK Bloggers. *The International Journal of the Book*, 5(1).

Conclusions

The aim of this book was to investigate the motivations of the average blogger. Looking mainly at personal rather than corporate blogs, it focused on the basic question: why blog?

There are many possible motivations put forward by academic researchers, the mainstream media and bloggers themselves. Bloggers wish to contribute to public debate; they use their blogs to vent about both public affairs and personal issues; they work through issues in their own lives and seek support from their readership; and they can use their blogs to make friends, make money, make sense of information and make a name for themselves.

Blogging can be a form of online diary-writing. There is much that is diary-like about a blog – its chronological structure; its potential for a focus on the writer and his or her experiences and feelings. Such journal blogs are particularly attractive to women bloggers – indeed blogs have been described as the traditionally feminine act of diary-writing, meeting the traditionally masculine world of ICT, and it was noticeable that the idea of the blog as diary was slightly more popular with our women survey respondents than the men. Men are more likely to blog about external events, rather than personal ones, which has been suggested as one reason for their popularity and overall dominance in the blogosphere. However, it may be that, by combining online communication with the more traditional genre, a blog offers men the opportunity to experience diary-writing without the feminine connotations of a traditional diary.

However, blogging is more than diary-writing because blogging is performed in the public gaze and with the benefits of Internet technology. While the respondents to our surveys understood the concept of the blog as an online diary, they did not exclusively think of their blogging in such terms. Respondents rarely chose just one definition of blogging when offered the descriptions of diary-writing, publishing, journalism and other. They saw blogging as a combination of at least two of these, and the majority of respondents selected all three of the descriptions offered.

A blog has an external audience: it is not just written for the benefit of the author, but also offers the possibilities of communication with others, often in similar situations to that of the blogger. It is noticeable that comment-writers on blogs are frequently similarly situated and therefore feel an instant connection to the blogger's experience. This audience does not have to read the blog in a conventional chronological way, as one would read a traditional paper diary. With the use of archives, the search function, links and other categorisation aids that might be offered by the blogger, the reader can navigate through the blog in a variety of different ways, creating their own paths through, away from and back to the current blog post. Thus Internet technology offers the reader a more fluid reading experience than the static traditional diary. In addition, blogs sit on the cusp of the private and public sphere – part of the public sphere and yet based within the privacy of the blogger's own website and offering the blogger the ability to edit, censor or cut any comments or postings (their own or others') that they do not like.

Thus while the description of blogs as online diaries can be a useful quick definition, most bloggers see blogging as more than this. And it should also be noted that online diarists draw a sharp distinction between themselves and bloggers. While online diarists might make use of blogs for immediate, spontaneous notes and impressions, they use their online diaries for more formal and considered writing. Blogs are seen as a more immediate genre – collecting a writer's impressions of events or emotions almost while they happen.

Thus blogs can fulfil a diary function for their writers, and yet because they are publicly available for other readers they are both more and less than a diary. They are not fully private, although the blogger is in control of what is allowed to be written in the blog, and they offer the possibilities not just of an audience, but an audience that might respond with comments and feedback. Bloggers who start their blog with the intention of keeping it as a diary can find that it develops away from the original diary form because of such feedback and they can quickly come to appreciate the extra benefits that come from having a responsive readership:

> Before my blog was used as an online journal of my daily life, this has now become a minor part of the blog and I am now mainly concentrating on technical issues and issues about blogging itself. This change has taken place as I realised I'd like more people to visit my site, which wasn't happening with the diary blog. (*Female respondent*, 2006)

However, even with the added attractions of an audience it should be noted that many bloggers still claim to be writing primarily for their own benefit. Journal blogs in particular often contain apologies to the blogger's readers for a particularly self-reflective or ranting post, while reminding readers that the blog was primarily set up for the benefit of the blogger. Events or relationships may not be fully explained because the blogger is not writing primarily for the reader and therefore feels little need to offer explanatory descriptions. With such posts bloggers might also be distinguishing between the general reader, who is not intimate with the blogger, and those readers who are also offline friends and are thus able to fill in the missing detail between the lines of such sketchy posts.

This leads us to consider the way in which blogging can be psychologically beneficial. Bloggers can be motivated to blog because of a desire to deepen their understanding of themselves and because it helps them to cope with events in their lives. The use of self-reflective writing in order to understand and learn from experiences can be linked to both traditional diary-keeping and more modern psycho-therapeutic practices where clients are encouraged to write down their experiences in order to explore them in depth. We have noted, for example, that the Internet offers a safe space within which bloggers can discuss their own sexuality and that sex blogging is represented in the mainstream media as particularly associated with women bloggers (although it can be disapproved of in the wider blogosphere as a cheap trick to raise a blogger's profile). Thus a blog can offer a safe place in which a blogger can explore his or her inner psyche, but with the added benefit that its public nature offers the possibility of communication with and support from others. This support might come from total strangers – and some bloggers are attracted to the idea of discussing personal issues with someone who does not know them and will never meet them – or from offline friends and family. A blog can be a structured and indirect way in which to discuss problems with people a blogger knows in real life. It means that the blogger is in control of what is said and offers the possibility of avoiding direct, face-to-face confrontation. Thus distress and emotional need can be a motivating factor for some people to start blogging, and the support and friendship they find online can motivate them to continue.

The formation and nurturing of social relationships can also be a strong motivating factor in starting and continuing a blog. When discussing friendship as a motivator for blogging, some commentators distinguish between intrinsic and extrinsic motivators. Thus, some bloggers start to blog in order to find new friends on the Internet, whilst others blog in order to maintain friendships already formed elsewhere. Many people start blogging at the urging of their friends who are already online or in order to keep in touch with family and friends who might be geographically distant – the explanation for the many expat and 'gap year' blogs that can be found. It is suggested the women, in particular, have taken their traditional role as the communication hubs in a household online and now use Internet tools such as blogs and e-mail in order to keep in contact with distant family and friends. But blogging can also be used to establish new friendships and assuage loneliness. Bloggers writing about a particular subject that interests them – whether it be parenting, bird-watching or their religious beliefs – can use the Internet to communicate with others with similar interests, which might not be possible for them offline. Indeed, some bloggers prefer to communicate with strangers online – having a relationship 'on your own terms' also offers the possibility of staying in control of the friendship – and are uncomfortable with the idea of people they know reading their blog. This can sometimes lead to censorship of the blog or even its cessation.

Another way in which blogging can be psychologically beneficial is the way in which it offers bloggers the possibility of venting or 'blowing off steam' about either public affairs or personal issues. Again, blogs can be seen as a safe space in which to rant about upsetting or irritating problems – and here an audience can be especially appreciated. Letting off steam about problems can be both cathartic and useful and can be a major benefit of blogging. Thus mommy blogs allow mothers to offer a 'warts and all' picture of the realities of parenthood while pseudonymous academic blogs allow lecturers to rant about their students or their managers. However, the sense of security and a safe space in which to make these complaints may be a false one. Bloggers have been 'dooced' (sacked or disciplined for their blogging); criminals have been tracked down through their blogs and bloggers are now much more aware of the fact that their blogs may be searched by current or future employers and used in evidence against them. While much of the 'venting' to be found in the blogosphere is related to personal issues, there are also links to be found here with another oft-mentioned forerunner of the blog – the letter to the newspaper editor or the opinion column. Bloggers, and as we have seen particularly male bloggers, can be attracted to blogging because it offers them an opportunity to publish their opinion on topical news, possibly offering a different perspective or more in-depth material than is offered by the mainstream media. Such posts do not pretend to objectivity, indeed many bloggers celebrate their subjectivities, but represent the personal opinion and emotions of the blogger.

One of the most familiar images of the blogger that we find in the mainstream media is that of the 'citizen journalist', hoping to redress perceived distortions or failures in the news media and acting as part of a 'fifth estate'. This is also a depiction with which our survey respondents were familiar – over half of all respondents agreed that blogging was a form of journalism. However, despite this identification, only a minority of our survey respondents described their own blogs in such terms. For the majority, blogging about external, political, events took second place to blogging about their own lives and experiences. It thus seems that, despite the coverage in the mainstream media about citizen journalists and the impact and importance of political bloggers, these remain a small sub-section of the blogosphere. Our respondents' view of blogging as a form of journalism seems to have been influenced by media coverage of A-list blogs' perceived news-agendas and blogs provided by the mainstream media itself rather than their own personal experience of blogging, and it thus seems that for the average blogger, blogging is more to do with personal communication than with campaigning journalism.

However, whilst only a minority of bloggers consider themselves to be acting as journalists, far more are open to the idea that they might be publishers, and the use of a blog in order to practise and display a blogger's creative writing skills was a popular motivation. The conception of blogging as creative writing was particularly popular with the American respondents to the 2007 survey, and it was possible to make a distinction between them and British respondents, who associated blogging more with information technology tools and skills. This idea of the blog as a portfolio for a blogger's creative writing skills was linked to the hope that, through their blog, a blogger might be discovered by a publisher and be offered a contract. Such ambitions are not groundless – the example of the success of a blogger like Belle de Jour demonstrates that publishers do monitor popular blogs and that publishing opportunities can arise in this way. Indeed, the blog turned book is now such a frequent phenomenon that it has its own term – the blook. While successes such as *Diary of a Call-Girl* and *A Wife in the North* are not the norm, and the majority of bloggers have to content themselves with the appreciation of their blog's readership, a blog does offer the real potential to be a place where creative writing can be displayed and commented upon.

The possibilities of financial reward offered by blogging encompass not just the publishing of the blog in book form but also included hosting advertising, selling subscriptions, the marketing of a blogger's products and services or even selling a successful blog to a larger media company. A growing motivation in the blogosphere is connected to money, and this might be a particularly attractive motivator for bloggers based in the home, for example those who are caring for others, retired or unemployed. Blogs focused on particular subjects, such as parenting, have been attractive to advertisers since they can deliver a focused, loyal and financially responsible readership. However, such money-making may be criticised by others in the blogosphere – we have seen how many mommy bloggers have been particularly attacked for their collaboration with advertisers. It is interesting to note that women bloggers can be attacked in the blogosphere for writing both blogs that are too boring (mommy blogs) and those that are too titillating (sex blogs), suggesting that the satisfactions such women bloggers find in blogging must be strong enough to inspire them to ignore such criticisms.

Financial motivation is now such a motivator for one section of the blogosphere that in its latest report on the state of the blogosphere Technorati distinguished between what it termed 'hobbyist' bloggers and those who desired to at least partly supplement their income by blogging (Technorati, 2009). Many of our survey respondents expected to at least cover their blogging expenses, mostly through hosting advertising, and some were using their blogs to market goods and services. A select few were even professional bloggers, relying on their blogging skills to provide their entire income. It was noticeable that the majority of these respondents were female, and many were operating out of their own homes, hoping to augment the household income through their blogging.

Thus bloggers might be inspired to blog to find friends, to stay in touch with friends and family, for emotional support, to explore their inner psyche or sexuality, to vent their anger, to make their opinions and their writing skills known more widely or even to make money. What is important to note is that few bloggers had only one motivation. The majority of bloggers are motivated by a mixture of such motivations, just as the majority perceived blogging as a mixture of diary-writing, publishing, journalism and other definitions. And motivations might change over time, just as a blog might change. For example, diary blogs can become less introspective as the blogger starts to appreciate the feedback they are receiving from their readership, or filter blogs can become more personal as the blogger starts to enjoy displaying their writing skills. Some motivations, such as the use of the blog as a therapeutic tool, may only gradually dawn on the blogger and so may be more a motivation for continuing to blog rather than to start blogging in the first place. Blogging takes time, perseverance and commitment, and so in order for a blog to continue a blogger needs to find strong satisfaction and personal fulfilment in their blogging. While motivations differ from blogger to blogger, it does seem that in general women are more motivated by a desire to communicate with others while male bloggers find greater satisfaction than women in blogging to share their expertise, opinions and knowledge, and to find and share information. American men, in particular, found great satisfaction in demonstrations of their knowledge, wisdom or expertise, and their satisfaction in blogging appears to be related to their dominance in the Anglophone blogosphere.

However, as we have seen, there are bloggers who blog not because they want to or because they find great satisfaction in blogging but because they are told to blog as part of their job. We have seen that the mainstream media has now embraced blogging and that many newspapers and organisations such as the BBC now offer a variety of blogs by their reporters and columnists where they are able to write in a more personal and opinionated way, albeit still as employees of the company. In other words, the mainstream media is attempting to normalise blogging as an extension of journalism. However, while some journalists have been happy to embrace this opportunity, others have been less enthusiastic and motivation is a key factor in how committed such journalists can be to their blogs. As the research of Schultz and Sheffer demonstrated, those who were motivated to blog by their management rather than their own inclinations were more reluctant and less committed to blogging. To avoid this problem, some blogs have been 'bought in' by the newspapers rather than relying on their own journalists to start blogging.

A similar need for commitment can be found when blogs are used as educational or knowledge management tools. It is not enough for a lecturer or a manager to instruct their students or employees to start a blog. The blogger must find his or her blog personally useful in some way – perhaps as a tool for information management, as a way to communicate informally with others, as a support or as a way of showcasing their work – in order to be fully committed to the project. Blogging cannot be imposed from above; its benefits have to be clear in order for blogging to be enthusiastically taken up. And managers and lecturers need to be open to the possibility that their students and employees may find different benefits from blogging than the ones that are expected. The flexibility of blogging must be acknowledged – different bloggers make different uses and find different satisfactions from blogging.

Bloggers also adapt their blogging habits as change occurs. Thus Technorati's latest survey of the state of the blogosphere in 2009 found that bloggers were far more likely than the general population to make use of the new micro-blogging phenomenon of Twitter. While 14 per cent of the general population uses Twitter at present, 73 per cent of the blogging respondents to Techorati's survey did so. Why did they use it?

To promote their blog, bring interesting links to light and to know what people are talking about. In other words it seems that the uses that these bloggers made of Twitter was to augment their blogging rather than to replace it.

Thus the key points to be understood from this project are that blogs are flexible and changeable: their usefulness and the satisfactions to be gained from blogging can alter over time as a blogger's circumstances and needs change. They require commitment – the blogger must find his or her own satisfactions from blogging, it cannot be imposed from above. Bloggers are motivated to blog for a wide variety and mix of reasons – a need for support, communication, validation, to share expertise and knowledge, as an information management tool, as part of their job, even for financial recompense. What is clear is their enthusiasm for blogging and the many satisfactions they find in it. Perhaps the question should not be, why blog? But rather, why not?

Bibliography

Adamic, L.A. and Glance, N. (2005) 'The political blogosphere and the 2004 US election – divided they blog' in LinkKDD '05: *Proceedings of the 3rd International Workshop on Link Discovery*, pp. 36–43.

Ali-Hasan, N.F. and Adamic, L.A. (2007) 'Expressing social relationships on the Blog through links and comments', International Conference on Weblogs and Social Media. Boulder: ICWSM *http://www.icwsm.org/papers/2-Ali-Hasan-Adamic.pdf* (accessed on 9 March 2010)

Allen, K. and Rainie, L. (2002) *Pew Internet and American Life Project Report: Family, friends and community*, 'Parents Online'. 17 November 2002.

Attwood, F. (2009) 'Intimate adventures: Sex blogs, sex "blooks" and women's sexual narration', *European Journal of Cultural Studies*, 12(1): 5–20.

Baikie, K.A. and Wilhelm, K. (2005) 'Emotional and physical health benefits of expressive writing', *Advances in Psychiatric Treatment*, 11: 338–46.

Baker, J. and Moore, S. (2008) 'Distress, coping and blogging: Comparing New MySpace users by their intention to blog', *CyberPsychology and Behavior*, 11(1): 81–5.

Bar-Ilan, J. (2005) 'Information hub blogs: A uses and gratifications inquiry into bloggers' motivations', *Journal of Information Science*, 31(4): 297–307.

Beetham, M. (2006) 'Periodicals and the new media: Women and imagined communities', *Women's Studies International Forum*, 29(3), 231–40.

Bentley, C., Hamman, B., Littau, J., Meyer, H., Watson, B. and Welsh, B. (2007) 'Citizen journalism: A case study' in Tremayne, M. (ed.), *Blogging, Citizenship and the Future of Media*. New York and London: Routledge, pp. 239–59.

Blood, R. (2004) 'How blogging software reshaped the online community', *Communications of the ACM*, December 2004. *http://www.rebeccablood.net/essays/blog_software.html* (accessed on 9 February 2010).

Boneva, B. and Kraut, R. (2002) 'E-mail, gender and personal relationships' in Wellman, B. and Haythornthwaite, C. (eds), *The Internet in Everyday Life*. Oxford: Blackwell, pp. 372–403.

boyd, d. (2005a). 'Broken metaphors: Blogging as liminal practice', Paper presented at Media Ecology Conference, New York, NY.

boyd, d. (2005b) 'Zapophenia' Why so many teenage girls? [comment]. lj_research, 30 April 2005. *http://community.livejournal.com/lj_research/17767.html* (accessed on 20 September 2005).

boyd, d. (2006) 'Identity production in a networked culture: Why youth heart MySpace' [unpublished talk], American Association for the Advancement of Science, February 19, 2006. *http://www.danah.org/papers/AAAS2006.html* (accessed on 13 March 2006).

Brady, M. (2006) 'Blogs – motivations behind the phenomenon', Chimera Working Paper, No. 2006–17. *http://www.essex.ac.uk/chimera/content/pubs/wps/CWP-2006-17-blog-motivations.pdf* (accessed on 9 February 2010).

Brooke, S. (5 July 2009) 'Sold to the Highest Blogger', *The Times*. *http://property.timesonline.co.uk/tol/life_and_style/property/buying_and_selling/article6632742.ece* (accessed on 5 July 2009).

Buell, E.H. (1975) 'Eccentrics or gladiators? People who write about politics in letters to the editor', *Social Science Quarterly*, 56: 440–9.

Burkeman, O. (2005) 'The new commentariat', *Guardian Unlimited*, 17 November 2005. *http://www.guardian.co.uk/g2/story/0,,1644298,00.html* (accessed on 17 November 2005).

Caesar, E. (2006) 'Meet the bloggerati', *The Independent Online Edition*, 20 March 2006. *http://news.independent.co.uk/media/article352287.ece* (accessed on 21 March 2006).

Chancellor, A. (2003) 'Sometimes it's hard to be a woman', *The Guardian: Weekend Comment and Features*, 8 November 2003, p. 9.

Chandler, D. (1998) 'Personal home pages and the construction of identities on the Web'. *http://www.aber.ac.uk/media/Documents/short/webident.html* (accessed on 8 August 2009).

Chun-Yao, H., Yong-Zheng, S., Hong-Xiang, L. and Shin-Skin, C. (2007) 'Bloggers' motivations and behaviours: A model', *Journal of Advertising Research*, 47(4): 472–84.

Cohen, N. (2007) 'Meet Colby Buzzell, a king among blookers', *The Observer*, 6 May 2007, p. 12.

Costa, P.T., Jr., and McCrae, R.R. (1992) 'Normal personality assessment in clinical practice: The NEO personality inventory', *Psychological Assessment* 4: 5–13, quoted in Guadagno, R.E., Okdie, B.M. and

Eno, C.A. (2008) 'Who blogs? Personality predictors of blogging', *Computers in Human Behavior*, 24(5): 1993–2004.

De Almeida Soares, D. (2008) 'Understanding class blogs as a tool for language development', *Language Teaching Research,* 12(4): 517–33.

Dickey, M.D. (2004) 'The impact of web-logs (blogs) on student perceptions of isolation and alienation in a web-based distance-learning environment', *Open Learning*, 19(3): 279–91.

van Doorn, N., van Zoonen, L. and Wyatt, S. (2007) 'Writing from experience: Presentations of gender identity on weblogs', *European Journal of Women's Studies,* 14: 143–59.

Drezner, H. and Farrell, D.W. (2008) 'The power and politics of blogs', *Public Choice*, 134: 15–30.

Duffy, P.D. and Bruns, A. (2006) 'The use of blogs, wikis and RSS in education – a conversation of possibilities', *Proceedings Online Learning and Teaching Conference*, Brisbane, 2006, pp. 31–8.

Efimova, L. (2003) 'Blogs: The stickiness factor', BlogTalk: A European Conference on Weblogs. Vienna, 23 May 2003. *https://doc.freeband .nl/dsweb/Get/Document34088/Blogs_stikiness_factor.pdf* (accessed on 9 February 2010).

Erwins, R. (2005) 'Who are you? Weblogs and academic identity', *E-learning*, 2(4). *http://www.wwwords.co.uk/pdf/freetoview.asp?j=ele a&vol=2&issue=4&year=2005&article=6_Ewins_ELEA_2_4_web* (accessed on 9 November 2009).

Fallows, D. (2005) 'How women and men use the Internet', Washington: Pew/Internet. Pew Internet & American Life Project, 28 December 2005. *http://www.pewinternet.org/pdfs/PIP_Women_and_Men_online .pdf* (accessed on 10 January 2006).

Feather, J. (2005) *History of British Publishing*. London: Routledge.

Forbes, T. (2009) 'Ethical dialogue and the changing communications landscape: Can blogs help corporations achieve public relations excellence by facilitating contingency interactivity?' Unpublished MSc thesis, The Robert Gordon University, Aberdeen.

Foster, H.S. and Friedrich, C.J. (1937) 'Letters to the editor as a means of measuring the effectiveness of propaganda', *American Political Science Review*, 31: 71–9.

Garfunkel, J. (2005) 'Promoting women bloggers: A timeline of relevant discussions', *Civilities media structures research* [blog]. *http://civilities .net/PromotingWomenBloggersTimeline* (accessed on 23 February 2006).

Gibb, F. (2009, 17 June) 'Ruling on NightJack author Richard Horton kills blogger anonymity', *The Times. http://technology.timesonline*

.co.uk/tol/news/tech_and_web/the_web/article6509677.ece (accessed on 30 September 2009).

Gillmor, D. (2006) *We the Media: Grassroots Journalism by the People, for the People* (2nd edn). Sebastopol, CA: O'Reilly.

Gregg, M. (2009) 'Banal Bohemia: Blogging from the ivory tower hot-desk', *Convergence,* 15(4): 470–83.

Grey, D.L. and Brown, T.B. (1970) 'Letters to the editor: Hazy reflections of public opinion', *Journalism Quarterly,* 47: 450–6, 471.

Grice, E. (2008) 'Northern Exposure: Wife in the North', *The Telegraph. http://www.telegraph.co.uk/portal/main.jhtml?xml=/portal/2008/07/05/ ftwifenorth105.xml* (accessed on 5 July, 2008).

Guadagno, R.E., Okdie, B.M. and Eno, C.A. (2008) 'Who blogs? Personality predictors of blogging', *Computers in Human Behavior,* 24(5): 1993–2004.

Gumbrect, M. (2004) 'Blogs as a "protected space"', presented at the *Workshop on the Weblogging Ecosystem: Aggregation, Analysis, and Dynamics: WWW 2004.* New York: ACM Press.

Gurak, L.J. and Antonijevic, S. (2008) 'The psychology of blogging – you, me and everyone in between', *American Behavioral Scientist,* 52: 60–8.

Hau-nung Chan, A. (2008) 'Life in Happy Land? – Using virtual space and doing motherhood in Hong Kong', *Gender, Place and Culture,* 15(2): 169–88.

Healy, R. (2007, March 9) 'Murder, they blogged', *Time Magazine. http:// www.time.com/time/nation/article/0,8599,1597801,00.html?cnn=yes* (accessed on 30 September 2009).

Henning, J. (2003) 'The blogging iceberg', Perseus. *http://www.perseus .com/blogsurvey/iceberg.html* (accessed on 5 October 2005).

Henning, J. (2005) 'Nothing old can stay', Perseus Blog Survey weblog, 23 December 2005. *http://www.perseusdevelopment.com/blogsurvey/ blog/051223agerange.html* (accessed on 8 March 2006).

Hermida, A. (2008) 'The BBC goes blogging – Is "Auntie" finally listening?' *http://online.journalism.utexas.edu/2008/papers/Hermida .pdf* (accessed on 19 October 2009).

Herring, S.C. and Paolillo, J.C. (2006) 'Gender and genre variation in weblogs', *Journal of Sociolinguistics,* 10(4): 439–59.

Herring, S.C., Kouper, I., Schiedt, L.A., and Wright, E.L. (2004a) 'Women and children last: The discursive construction of weblogs', *Into the Blogosphere. http://blog.lib.umn.edu/blogosphere/women_ and_children.html* (accessed on 7 March 2006).

Herring, S.C., Schiedt, L.A., Bonus, S., and Wright, E. (2004b) 'Bridging the gap: A genre analysis of weblogs', *Information, Technology &*

People, 18(2): 142–71. *http://www.blogninja.com/DDGDD04.doc* (accessed on 7 March 2006).

Herring, S.C. (1994) 'Gender differences in computer-mediated communication: Bringing familiar baggage to the new frontier', Keynote talk at the American Library Association Annual Conference, Miami, June 1994.

Hill, J. (2005) 'The voice of the blog: The attitudes and experiences of small business bloggers using blogs as a marketing and communications tool', unpublished MBA dissertation, University of Liverpool, England.

Hookway, N. (2008) 'Entering the blogosphere: Some strategies for using blogs in social research', *Qualitative Research*, 8(1): 91–113.

Huffaker, D.A. and Calvert, S.L. (2005) 'Gender, identity and language use in teenage blogs', *Journal of Computer-Mediated Communication*, 10(2). *http://jcmc.indiana.edu/vol10/issue2/huffaker.html* (accessed on 9 February 2010).

Huffaker, D. (2004) 'Gender similarities and differences in online identity and language use among teenage bloggers' MA thesis, Georgetown University. *http://cct.georgetown.edu/thesis/DavidHuffaker.pdf* (accessed on 3 June 2004).

Huffaker, D. (2005) 'The educated blogger – using weblogs to promote literacy in the classroom', *AACE Journal*, 13(2): 91–8.

Jackson, N. (2008)'Representation in the blogosphere: MPs and their new constituents', *Parliamentary Affairs*, 61(4): 642–60.

Jalland, P. (1986) *Women, Marriage and Politics 1860–1914*. Oxford: Clarendon Press.

Kahn, R. and Kellner, D. (2004) 'New media and Internet activism: From the "Battle of Seattle" to blogging', *New Media & Society*, 6(1): 87–95.

Karlsson, L. (2003) 'Consuming lives, creating community, female Chinese-American diary writing on the Web', *Prose Studies*, 26(1): 219–39.

Kawaura, Y., Kawakami, Y. and Yamashita, K. (1998) 'Keeping a diary in cyberspace', *Japanese Psychological Research*, 40: 234–45.

Kaye, B.K. (2007) 'Blog use motivations – an exploratory study' in Tremayne, M. (ed.), *Blogging, Citizenship and the Future of Media*. New York and London: Routledge, pp. 127–48.

Kerawalla, L., Minocha, S., Kirkup, G. and Conole, G. (2008) 'Characterising the different blogging behaviours of students on an online distance learning course', *Learning, Media and Technology*, 33(1): 21–33.

Kerawalla, L., Minocha, S., Kirkup, G. and Conole, G. (2009). 'An empirically grounded framework to guide blogging in higher education', *Journal of Computer Assisted Learning*, 25(1): 31–42.

Kerr, O.S. (2006) 'Blogs and the legal academy', *Washington University Law Review*, 84: 1127–43.

Krause, S.D. (2005, June 24) 'Blogs as a tool for teaching', *The Chronicle of Higher Education*, 51(42): B33.

Krishnamurthy, S. (2002) 'The multidimensionality of blog conversations: the virtual enactment of September 11', Paper presented at Internet Research 3.0, Maastricht, The Netherlands.

Kumar, R., Novak, J., Raghavan, P. and Tomkins, A. (2004) 'Structure and evolution of blogspace', *Communications of the ACM*, 47(12): 35–9.

Lander, B.G. (1972) 'Functions of letters to the editor: A re-examination', *Journalism Quarterly*, 49: 142–3.

Lenhart, A. and Madden, M. (2005) 'Teen content creators and consumers', Washington: Pew/Internet (Pew Internet & American Life Project, 2 November 2005). *http://www.pewinternet.org.pdfs/PIP_Teens_Content_Creation.pdf* (accessed on 14 November 2005).

Lenhart, A. and Fox, S. (2006) 'Bloggers: Pew Internet and American Life Project'. *http://www.pewinternet.org/Reports/2006/Bloggers.aspx* (accessed on 9 February 2010).

Lopez, L.K. (2009). 'The radical act of "mommy blogging": Redefining motherhood through the blogosphere', *New Media and Society*, 11: 729–47.

Lowrey, W. and Anderson, W. (2005) 'The journalist behind the curtain: Participatory functions on the internet and their impact on perceptions of the work of journalism', *Journal of Computer-Mediated Communication*, 10(3): article 13. *http://jcmc.indiana.edu/vo0l10/issue3/lowrey.html* (accessed on 14 November 2006).

Madge, C. and O'Connor, H. (2006) 'Parenting gone wired – empowerment of new mothers on the Internet', *Social and Cultural Geography*, 7(2): 199–220.

Matheson, D. (2004) 'Weblogs and the epistemology of the news: Some trends in online journalism', *New Media and Society*, 6(4): 443–68.

McCarthy, Z. (2007) *My Boyfriend is a Twat*. London: The Friday Project.

McNeill, L. (2005) 'Genre under construction – the diary on the Internet', *Language@Internet*, 2. *http://www.languageatinternet.de/articles/2005/120* (accessed on 9 February 2010).

Menchen-Trevino, E. (2005) 'Blogger motivations: power, pull and positive feedback.' Unpublished thesis, University of Illinois, Chicago.

Miller, H.W. and Mather, R. (1998) 'The presentation of self in WWW home pages', Paper presented at IRISS 98 Conference, Bristol.

Miura, A. and Yamashita, K. (2007) 'Psychological and social influences on blog writing: An online survey of blog authors in Japan.' *Journal of Computer-Mediated Communication*, 12(4): article 15. *http://jcmc.indiana.edu/vol12/issue4/miura.html* (accessed on 9 February 2010).

Miyata, K. (2002) 'Social support for Japanese mothers online and offline' in Wellman, B. and Haythornthwaite, C. (eds), *The Internet in Everyday Life*. Oxford: Blackwell, pp. 520–48.

Mortensen, T. and Walker, J. (2002) 'Blogging thoughts: Personal publication as an online research tool' in Morrison, A. (ed.), *Researching ICTs in Context*. InterMedia Report, 3/2002, Oslo.

Murthy, D. (2008) 'Digital ethnography – an examination of the use of new technologies for social research', *Sociology*, 42(5): 837–55.

Nardi, B., Schiano, D., Gumbrecht, M. and Swartz, L. (2004a) 'Why we blog', *Communications of the ACM*, 47(12): 41–6.

Nardi, B.A., Schiano, D.J., Gumbrecht, M. and Swartz, L. (2004b) '"I'm blogging this": A closer look at why people blog', *Communications of the ACM*, December 2004. *http://home.comcast.net/~diane.schiano/Blog.draft.pdf* (accessed 8 February 2010).

Newson, A., Houghton, D. and Patten, J. (2009) *Blogging and other social media – exploiting the technology and protecting the enterprise*. Farnham: Gower.

Nielsen/Net Ratings. (2007) 'Young women now the most dominant group online'. *http://www.nielsen-netratings.com/* (accessed on 8 January 2008).

Nowell, B. (2009) 'Free digital content: Commercial or cannibal? How trade publishers are using free digital content to promote sales'. Unpublished MA dissertation, University College, London.

Ojala, M. (2005) 'Blogging for knowledge sharing, management and dissemination', *Business Information Review*, 22(4): 269–76.

Oravec, J. (2003) 'Blending by blogging – weblogs in blended learning initiatives', *Journal of Educational Media*, 28(2–3): 225–33.

O'Sullivan, C. (2005) 'Diaries, online diaries and the future loss to archives – or, blogs and the blogging bloggers who blog them', *The American Archivist*, 68: 53–73.

Palko, A (2007) 'Poaching the print: Theorising the scrapbook in Stephen King's *Misery*', *International Journal of the Book*, 4(3): 59–62.

Papacharissi, Z. (2002) 'The self online: The utility of personal home pages', *Journal of Broadcasting and Electronic Media*, 46(3): 346–68.

Papacharissi, Z. (2007) 'Audiences as media producers: Content analysis of 260 blogs' in Tremayne, M. (ed.), *Blogging, Citizenship and the Future of Media*. New York and London: Routledge, pp. 21–38.

Pedersen, S. (2002a) 'A surfeit of socks? The impact of the First World War on women correspondents to daily newspapers', *Scottish Economic and Social History*, 22(1): 50–72.

Pedersen, S. (2002b, July) 'Within their sphere? Women correspondents to Aberdeen daily newspapers 1900–1914', *Northern Scotland*, pp. 159–66.

Pedersen, S. (2004) 'What's in a name? The revealing use of noms de plume in women's correspondence to daily newspapers in Edwardian Scotland', *Media History*, 10(3): 175–85.

Pedersen, S. (2007) 'Speaking the same language? Differences and similarities between US and UK bloggers', *The International Journal of the Book*, 5(1): 33–40.

Pedersen, S. (2008) 'Now read this: Male and female bloggers' recommendations for further reading', *Particip@tions: Journal of Audience and Reception Research*, 5(2). *http://www.participations .org/Volume%205/Issue%202/5_02_pedersen.htm* (accessed on 9 February 2010)

Pedersen, S. and Chivers, A. (2007) 'Readers' use of news blogs,' *International Journal of Technology, Knowledge and Society*, 3(1): 15–24.

Pedersen, S. and Macafee, C. (2006) 'The practices and popularity of British bloggers' in Martens, B. and Dobreva, M. (eds), *Digital Spectrum: Integrating Technology and Culture* (Proceedings of the 10th International Conference on Electronic Publishing held in Bansko, Bulgaria 14–16 June 2006). Vienna: ÖKK-Editions, pp. 155–64.

Pedersen, S. and Smithson, J. (2010) 'Membership and activity in an online parenting community', *Handbook of Research on Discourse Behavior and Digital Communication: Language Structures and Social Interaction*. Hershey, PA: IGI Global.

Pedley, P. (2005) 'International phenomenon? Amateur journalism? Legal minefield? Why information professionals cannot afford to ignore weblogs', *Business Information Review*, 22(2): 95–100.

Pennebaker, J.W. and Beall, S.K. (1986) 'Confronting a traumatic event: Toward an understanding of inhibition and disease', *Journal of Abnormal Psychology*, 95: 274–81.

Pollard, D. (2003) 'Is the blogosphere sexist? *How to save the world* [blog]'. *http://blogs.salon.com?0002007/2003/10/30.html* (accessed 9 March 2006).

Pounds, G. (2006) 'Democratic participation and letters to the editor in Britain and Italy', *Discourse and Society*, 17(29): 29–63.

Raeymaeckers, K. (2005) 'Letters to the editor: A feedback opportunity turned into a marketing tool,' *European Journal of Communication*, 20(2): 199–221.

Ratliff, C. (2004a) 'Whose voices get heard? Gender politics in the blogosphere', *Culture Cat* [blog]. *http://culturecat.net/node/303* (accessed 12 September 2005).

Ratliff, C. (2004b) '*The* link portal on gender in the blogosphere', *Culture Cat* [blog]. *http://culturecat.net/node/637* (accessed 12 September 2006).

Ratliff, C. (2006). WATW by the numbers. *Culture Cat* [blog]. *http://culturecat.net/node/1030* (accessed 21 March 2006).

Reader, B. (2008). 'Turf wars? Rhetorical struggle over "prepared" letters to the editor', *Journalism*, 9(5): 606–23.

Reed, A. (2005) " 'My blog is me": Texts and persons in UK online journal culture (and anthropology)', *Ethnos*, 70(2): 220–42.

Riley, D. (2005) 'Blog count for July: 70 million blogs. The Blog Herald', *b5media*. *http://www.blogherald.com/2005/07/19/blog-count-for-july-70-million-blogs/* (accessed 4 January 2006).

Sarkadi, A. and Bremberg, S. (2005) 'Socially unbiased parenting support on the Internet – a cross-sectional study of users of a large Swedish parenting website', *Child: Care, Health and Development*, 31(1): 43–52.

Schiano, D.J., Nardi, B.A., Gumbrecht, M. and Swartz, L. (2004, April 24–29) 'Blogging by the Rest of Us', *CHI 2004*. Vienna, Austria.

Schultz, B. and Sheffer, M.L. (2007) 'Sports journalists who blog cling to traditional values', *Newspaper Research Journal*, 28(4): 62–76.

Selwyn, N. (2008) 'An investigation of differences in undergraduates' academic use of the Internet', *Active Learning in Higher Education*, 9(11): 11–22.

Serfaty, V. (2004) *The Mirror and the Veil – An overview of American online diaries and blogs*. Amsterdam: Rodopi, Amsterdam Monographs of American Studies.

Shirky, C. (2008) *Here Comes Everybody*. London: Penguin.

Showalter, E. (ed) (1989) *Speaking of Gender*. London: Routledge.

Sifry, D. (2005). 'State of the blogosphere, August 2005, Part 1: Blog growth. Sifry's Alerts [blog]', *http://www.sifry.com/alerts/archives/000332.html* (accessed on 6 January 2006).

Sifry, D. (2006) 'State of the blogosphere, February 2006, Part 1: on blogosphere growth. Sifry's Alerts [blog], 6 February 2006', *http://www.sifry.com/alerts/archives/000419.html* (accessed on 23 February 2006).

Singer, J.B. (2005) 'The Political J-Blogger: Normalising a new media form to fit old norms and practices', *Journalism*, 6(2): 173–98.

Singh, T., Veron-Jackson, L. and Cullinane, J. (2008) 'Blogging: A new play in your marketing game plan', *Business Horizons*, 51: 281–92.

Smith, K.C., McLeod, K. and Wakefield, M. (2005) 'Australian letters to the editor on tobacco: Triggers, rhetoric and claims of legitimate voice', *Qualitative Health Research*, 15(9): 1180–98.

Spender, D. (1980) *Man Made Language*. London, Boston and Henley: Routledge and Kegan Paul.

Stefanone M.A. and Jang, C-Y. (2007) 'Writing for friends and family – the interpersonal nature of blogs', *Journal of Computer-Mediated Communication*, 13(1): article 7.

Technorati (2009) 'State of the blogosphere 2009'. *http://technorati.com/blogging/feature/state-of-the-blogosphere-2009/* (accessed on 9 February 2010).

Thelwall, M. (2006, May) 'Bloggers during the London attacks: Top information sources and topics', Paper presented at the 15th International World Wide Web Conference, Edinburgh, Scotland. *http://www.blogpulse.com/www2006-workshop/papers/blogs-during-london-attacks.pdf* (accessed on 5 May 2006).

Thelwall, M., Byrne, A., and Goody, M. (2007) 'Which types of news story attract bloggers?' *Information Research*, 12(4): paper 327.

Thelwall, M. and Stuart, D. (2007) 'RUOK? Blogging communication technologies during crises', *Journal of Computer-Mediated Communication*, 12(2): article 9.

Trammell, K.D., Tarkowski, A., Hofmokl J. and Sapp, A.M. (2006) 'Rzeczpospolita blogów [Republic of blog]: Examining Polish bloggers through content analysis', *Journal of Computer-Mediated Communication*, 11: 702–22.

Turkle, S. (1995). *Life on the Screen: Identity in the Age of the Internet*. New York: Simon & Schuster.

Viégas, F.B. (2005) 'Bloggers' Expectations of Privacy & Accountability', *Journal of Computer Mediated Communication*, 10(3): article 12.

Volgy, T.J. et al. (1977) 'Some of my best friends are letter writers: Eccentrics and gladiators revisited', *Social Science Quarterly*, 58: 321–27.

Wahl-Jorgensen, K. (2002) 'The construction of the public in letters to the editor: Deliberative democracy and the idiom of insanity', *Journalism*, 3(2): 183–204.

Walker, J. (2005) 'Mirrors and shadows – the digital pseudonymous aestheticization of oneself', *Proceedings of Digital Arts and Culture*, IT University Copenhagen, December 2005.

Walker, J. (2006) 'Blogging from inside the Ivory Tower', in Bruns, A. and Jacobs, J. (eds), *Uses of Blogs*. Peter Lang: New York.

Walker, K. (2000) 'It's difficult to hide it: The presentation of self on Internet home pages', *Qualitative Sociology*, 23(1): 99–120.

Wall, M. (2005) 'Blogs of War', *Journalism*, 6(2): 153–72.

White, R. (2007) 'Meet blook, son of blog, on the new frontier of publishing', *The Sunday Times*, 18 March 2007. *http://www .timesonline.co.uk/tol/news/uk/article1529873.ece.* (accessed on 9 February 2010).

Williams, J.B. and Jacobs, J. (2004) 'Exploring the use of blogs as learning spaces in the higher education sector', *Australasian Journal of Educational Technology*, 20(2): 232–47.

Williams Z. (2006) 'I don't write to titillate. I censor like crazy to make my blogs less erotic', *The Guardian*, 11 August 2006, p. 6

Wood, E.A. (2008) 'Consciousness-raising 2.0: Sex blogging and the creation of a feminist sex commons', *Feminism and Psychology*, 18: 480–87.

Woods, R. (2009). " '25 random things" confession craze sweeps the Internet', *The Times*, 15 February 2009.

Xifra, J. and Huertas, A. (2008) 'Blogging PR: An exploratory analysis of public relations weblogs', *Public Relations Review*, 34(3): 269–75.

Index

Breinigsville, PA USA
17 June 2010
240116BV00002B/1/P

9 781843 345831